A NEIGHBOUR KIND – AND KNOWN

Ambrose Tinsley OSB

A Neighbour
Kind – and Known

THE SPIRITUALITY OF
JULIAN OF NORWICH

the columba press

First published in 1997 by
the columba press
55a Spruce Avenue, Stillorgan Industrial Park
Blackrock, Co Dublin

Cover by Bill Bolger
Illustrations by Deirdre Humphries
Origination by The Columba Press
Printed in Ireland by Colour Books Ltd, Dublin

ISBN 1 85607 199 5

Contents

Foreword

Julian has become a favourite in recent years. To some extent, that is because she had an optimistic spirit and to some extent because she can encourage our own yearning for a life which secular society so often seems to thwart. For both those reasons I have come to like her too and now I hope that this, my contribution to the flow of books already published, will become for some at least an introduction to her thought.

What I am offering is just a number of short chapters, each of which reflects one of the major themes suggested or developed in her books. In dealing with them I have tried to keep the sequence of ideas which went through Julian's own mind on that occasion which I will refer to for convenience as her 'great experience' and which occurred when she was thirty-and-a-half. I have tried to respect as well the evolution of her thought, beginning with her very early prayers and then continuing through that same 'great experience' to the production of her first book and, then, to the two perceptible editions of her second one. I have, let it be said, accepted on intrinsic evidence the theory that her first book was what we refer to as the shorter one and that the longer version which we have was written when she was much older and had pondered on what God had seemed to say much more. We, therefore, can discern five stages as a framework for considering a possible maturing of her insights and her spiritual life.

However, I have let myself become a little bit creative too. I have imagined people coming to her anchorhold for help and have explored how her acceptance of those people may have helped her to appreciate the message of her 'great experience' and to express it in a way which made it relevant to all. This means, of course that even though I have tried to be always faithful to the thought of Julian some of my own ideas may have become confused with hers. Indeed one lady told me, after I had spoken about Julian, that she was not too sure where Julian's own thinking ceased and where my own began. I took it as a compliment and only hope that Julian, if she could read this book, would be prepared to say the same.

In any case, in offering these chosen themes I have begun each section with an introduction which puts each of them in context and refers the reader to those chapters in her own books in which they are chiefly found. Moreover, I have given at the end of almost every chapter some quotations from her books (either from her Long Text or her Short Text) and some verses from the scriptures which say much the same. My purpose was and is to lead the reader of this book into a period of reflection and of quiet prayer. That surely is what Julian herself would have desired.

However, may I add at this stage one brief word of gratitude to all who have in different ways helped me to write this book. My thanks to those who read and even re-read many times what I had written and for all the valuable comments an suggestions which they made. My thanks, especially, to Deirdre Humphries for providing illustrations to enhance each part of this work which I call *A Neighbour, Kind and Known*. That was what Julian had called St John of Beveley (LT chapter 38) but, in so doing, she was saying something which must surely have been true about herself as well.

Part One

Introducing Julian

The place of Julian's shrine today

Julian was born in 1342 (or possibly in 1343). While growing up she had a very strong devotion to the Crucified and, then, at thirty-and-a-half she had that 'great experience' in which she seemed to be participating in, not just his dying, but his exaltation too. For 20 years and more she pondered that remarkable event and all that it implied.

At some stage in her life she moved into an anchorhold. It was the anchorhold adjacent to the small church of St Julian (hence her name) and at the age of seventy she was still living there. Her life in such a place would certainly have been a silent one although it was the custom for the medieval anchorite or anchoress to speak with those who came for consultation or advice. It seems that Julian, while living for the most part in a solitary way, received such visitors from time to time and spoke with some of them about the mystery of Christ in which she had felt so involved. In any case it was from that small anchorhold in Norwich that her words have echoed down the ages and, quite obviously, are reverberating still.

What follows now is one approach to Julian and then a presentation of what seems to be the very essence of her message. After that, there is a brief description of her very dismal century, about which she says absolutely nothing – which of course makes what she does say all the more impressive.

WHO WAS SHE?

Many, many years ago, while browsing in a library, I came across a book by somebody called Julian of Norwich. I knew nothing of her at the time except that she had written some kind of a spiritual classic and, considering that it might do me good, I took it down and brought it to my room. But then, when I began to read it, my enthusiasm waned. It spoke so much of blood, of blood moreover which was red and warm! Although that blood was said to have been flowing from the wounds of Christ himself, it was at that time more than I could take and so I fairly quickly put the borrowed volume back.

Years passed, perhaps a quarter of a century, and then, quite unexpectedly, I found that Julian was trying, once again, to come into my life. This time, however, her attempt was to be more successful.

How it really started I cannot recall but something made me urge a small monastic study-group of which I was a member to accept her writings for reflection and discussion in the year that lay ahead. At first some of the others baulked at the idea. They said that Julian could hardly be considered a monastic author. I agreed that she was not a member of an organised community[1] but argued that her writings had become, in spite of that, a valuable part of the monastic and contemplative tradition of the church. It, consequently, was decided that we would accept her writings and allow her thought to mould our minds throughout the coming year. What none of us foresaw, however, was that that decision was to lead this present author to a love-affair with Julian which would last many years and is not over yet. It was a love-affair which has, in fact, done me a lot of good and I can only hope that Julian is not too disappointed.

Indeed, this time she really fascinated me. The passages about the warm and flowing blood, which had upset me in our first encounter, were no longer any problem. I could see quite clearly that in fact they occupied no more than just a tiny fraction of her book and that, in any case, when they occurred they very quickly led the reader to more satisfying lines. I, therefore, realised that all the blood which Julian described as flowing from the wounds of Christ had, even for herself, no more than relative importance. It revealed a deeper truth: that all the love which comes, or flows, from Christ can, not just cleanse us from all sin, but also fill with a new and everlasting life. That was the central point of Julian's own personal experience and of the message which she so desired to give.

As I began to study more and more the words of Julian I found myself attracted by the richness of her thought. But what impressed me most was her own underlying attitude to life. Although she lived in what from many points of view could be considered as a dismal and depressing age, her 'great experience' had filled her with a spirit of unfailing hope and so she could declare with confidence: 'all will be well'. She did not say, nor did she even know, how that could ever be but her conviction that it would be so must have encouraged many people of her time just as it has encouraged many others ever since. It is, of course, the only and inevitable outcome when one is convinced that God is good and full of what is both a wise and very powerful love.

As I continued studying the books of Julian what frequently intrigued me was the similarity between a number of her thoughts and those which are expressed in many parts of scripture. It is true that there are only two occasions[2] when she seems to quote directly what a sacred author actually wrote but there are many other places where an echo of what is contained in scripture can be heard. In fact this frequency so fascinated me that, in my preparations for an early meeting of our study-group, I spent a lot of time in drawing up a list of scripture-verses which could have inspired her thinking as she wrote. Indeed, it may have been at that same meeting that I volunteered the thought that Julian had been inspired by that same Spirit which, according to our Christian faith, had long before inspired the authors of the scriptures too. If that is true, and I believe it is, then Julian most certainly deserves a special place, not just in the monastic and contemplative tradition, but within the wider, lay tradition of the universal church as well.

Throughout the next few years I kept on reading Julian and pondering her thoughts. Some books about her were, in those days, being published too and many of them I obtained and studied on my own. Then I decided that the next thing I should do should be to make a pilgrimage to Norwich, to the very place where she herself had lived. I knew that, as a modern city, it would be extremely different to what it had been in the days of Julian herself but I confess that, when I reached it, I was charmed by the delightful, reconstructed church which occupies the very site where hers so long ago had been. It is a small attractive building and, on one side of the nave, there is a stone-cut, medieval doorway which leads to a simple room commemorating more or less the very spot where Julian, the anchoress, had dwelt.

I entered and, as I was sitting there, I tried to think of Julian in fourteenth-century England and of how she would have lived. Within the anchorhold itself (however it had been designed) her day would have been fairly ordered with specific times for prayer and reading and, no doubt, some other times for doing ordinary chores. But then I caught sight of a stained-glass window which was in the wall between me and that church from which I had just come and I surmised that, if there had been any opening there for Julian it would most probably have been a little lower down. That would have been to let her see the eucharist when it was being celebrated with the people in the church and to participate in other services as well.[3] In any case, that window made me think about that second one which she, like other anchoresses, would have had. That was the window through which she would welcome those who came to speak with her about their problems and to ask her for her prayers.[4] Although she was an anchoress, her prayerful life would not have been irrelevant to all the expectations and the needs of the society around.

I thought about her as a social asset for a while and tried to think of what she might have said to different people who consulted her. But time was passing by and soon I had to leave that quiet and inspiring spot and make my way back to the station for the train to London and the plane to bring me home. However, as I left, I bought some picture post-cards and some sketches which, I thought, might help to illustrate some lectures which I had agreed to give on my return. I even thought that, maybe, someday, they might help me in the writing of a book.

THE HEART OF THE MYSTERY

It was in 1373, on May the 13th (or the 8th)[5] that Julian experienced her 'Showings' as they have been often called. They happened when she was extremely sick and even close to death. Indeed her mother who was with her thought at one stage that she had in fact already died and, reaching out, was just about to close her eyes.[6] Yet Julian did not expire. She, suddenly and unexpectedly, revived. No doubt her mother and the others who had gathered there were both relieved and very grateful at that unexpected change. But what they did not know was that in those few harrowing hours the dying Julian experienced a presence which would influence the rest of her own life and, through her, those of many other people too.

The basic story is quite simply told. When Julian was thirty-and-a-half she caught a serious disease. She does not tell us what it was although some symptoms are described. In any case, her own condition worsened and the local curate came and, holding up a crucifix in front of her, said: 'I have brought an image of your saviour, look at it, take comfort from it.'[7] With a strange reluctance, Julian turned her eyes in its direction and, while darkness seemed to grow around her, on the image which was on the cross a strange and unexpected light began to shine. It was a little after that that she experienced within herself that sudden change which was to lead to her recovery and to a new and very fruitful life. It was as if the light which she saw shining on the Crucified was also penetrating and transforming her.

Perhaps, we can compare this personal experience of Julian to those of people who go to the very doors of death and say, when they return, that at that very moment they were also very conscious of some kind of presence and, quite frequently, of some attractive and consoling light as well.[8] A number of such near-to-death experiences have been recorded[9] and, because they come from people who are not attempting to impose a spiritual faith, they can encourage many others in their ordinary search. Those testimonies, therefore, are worth reading but, concerning Julian, they have an extra value: they may help us to perceive how her conviction of God's love for her was able to become so very strong.

Let me explain this by referring to a case which was not ever published but was privately disclosed to me.

It is about a person who was in a train which crashed and partly overturned. Although that person was not physically hurt, she had at that dramatic moment an experience which meant so much that, even after many years, she spoke of it as if it were but yesterday. She said that when the accident occurred the passengers were thrown in all directions as one would of course expect. But then she told me that, while that was happening, she had within herself a deep and very wonderful experience. She felt that she was loved as she had never been before, and more than she had ever thought was even possible. She had, more-over, an awareness of a presence which was very near, a pres-ence which she told me was that of her 'granny' who had died some years before and to whom she had been particularly close. Then, when the impact-moment passed and all the people in the train were trying hard to extricate themselves, she knew that some day, somehow, she would have that same experience again.

The case of Julian, I must concede, contained some elements which were quite different. Unlike the person in the train, she had been physically ill. Moreover, while the period of time in which my friend experienced such unexpected love was very brief, for Julian it lasted many hours. (It seems to have begun quite early in the morning and to have continued until sometime in mid-afternoon. Then, after some hours interval, it started once again and lasted for another while.) But, more importantly, my friend identified the loving presence with her 'granny', while for Julian, perhaps for reasons which can be explained, it was iden-tified with Christ. However, there are similarities as well: a near-to-death experience, a sense of being loved, a presence which can be expressed as light or love or both. Indeed these similarities would seem to outweigh any differences which we can find. Should we not, therefore, understand the core of Julian's own 'great experience' as being one such near-to-death experience, although of course there were within it other factors too?

But let us ask why Julian should link the loving presence in her own experience, not with some person who was known, a 'granny' for example, but with Christ. One reason could have been that since she had been very young her mind was focused strongly on the personality of Christ. She tells us that she even had a great desire to see him as those people did who had as-sembled near the cross when he was giving his own life for them.[10] A second reason could have been that in this focusing on Christ she was supported by a trend within society itself.[11] It was to see in him and in his passion the expression of a love

which can give meaning to our lives. Against that kind of background the appearance of a crucifix, especially to someone who
was sensitive, could have effectively suggested that the love
which we desire is linked, not (only) to a 'granny' or a parent recently deceased, but to the one who hung upon the cross and is,
as Julian herself perceived, a parent to us all. If that is why she
thought of Christ as mediating all the love which she seemed to
receive, all I will add is that, although so many circumstances
may be different, such an understanding of a deeply manifested
presence still occurs.[12]

Julian, in any case, revived and lived indeed for many
decades more. Perhaps, like some of those who speak about
their near-to-death experience, she also sensed that there was
still some work for her to do. Perhaps. In any case we might note
once again that she had no desire at all to gaze upon the crucifix
when it was being held before her face. Although she had
prayed as a young girl to be totally identified with Christ, a part
of her was obviously unprepared to be so when the crucial moment
came. That lack of willingness to contemplate and to accept the
crucified would re-emerge in days which were to come but we
might draw at least one tentative conclusion now. It is that, while
the deeper part of her desired to be enfolded in the all-embracing love of God, another part required more time before it could
accept a love which was expressed in such a crucifying way.

The fullness of that time would come but it would be through
living out her own particular vocation as a anchoress that she
would be prepared. It would, moreover, be through doing all
she could, within the context of her own vocation, to help others
both to know and to accept that love which God, through Christ,
is offering to all. It is that aspect of her own vocation, which in
some way has to be an aspect of our own as well, which needs
particular consideration now.

A LIGHT IN A DARKENED WORLD

It was a troubled and depressing age. The writings of that fourteenth century suggest an all-pervading sense of gloom and, if in
England there were glimmers of excitement as that country

struggled on to nationhood, the underlying fact is that the people there, as elsewhere, suffered in a lot of crucifying ways. Indeed, we could say that that period in history was, to use a famous phrase, 'the worst of times'[13] and many who were living then would possibly have thought so too. However, if we were to re-assess that century again and this time with a special eye on Julian, and others who were like her, we might be inclined to add the other half of that same famous phrase and say 'it was the best of times' as well. 'The worst of times!' 'The best of times!' Though Julian herself did not sum up the situation in that way she was, however, certain from her own experience that, even in the midst of great calamities, one could acquire not only peace and happiness but even moments of what she referred to as 'delight'.

However, for the moment let us focus on a few of those calamities which caused such sadness and depression at the time. But, as we do, it might not be a bad idea to keep in mind some of their counterparts today. We too are living in an age which could be called 'the worst of times' although of course in some ways it could also be considered as 'the best'.

The first calamity which ought to be considered was that long, if intermittent, war between the English and the French. It had in fact begun before the birth of Julian and it continued even after she had died. Perhaps it could be thought of as a symptom of a young, ambitious people but, like every other war, it would have caused the death of many and the sufferings of many more. Indeed, we can imagine the distress when news of husbands or of fathers killed in battle came back to their families at home. But let us here imagine too some members of those shattered families appearing at the window of the anchorhold of Julian. Perhaps, they only wanted to pour out their grief and felt that she was someone who would have a sympathetic and an understanding ear. No doubt she had but maybe not a few of those who came to her found consolation, not just in her presence, but in what she may have said to them as well.

The second great calamity which struck the people of that cen-

tury was that horrific plague which has become known by the
vivid and alarming name: 'Black Death'. It had originated in the
East and, when it had been brought to Europe, it spread rapidly
and, in the case of England, was to claim the lives of almost half
its population. When in 1349 it first appeared in Norwich, Julian
herself would have been no more than a child of seven but she
must have been aware, not just of people dying all around her,
but of the anxiety and fear which that mysterious and quickly-
killing illness would have caused. Indeed, the fear would have
been all the greater since those very people could have thought
that they would die without an opportunity to get a sacramental
absolution for their sins and so, it seemed to them, be damned.
However for a while the plague abated but in 1361 another
strain of it appeared and this time it was mostly children who
contracted it and died. That too must have been harrowing for
Julian who was by then a woman of nineteen and could indeed
have been a mother, too. Some people say she was. But even that
was not the end for there were further outbreaks in the years
ahead when Julian was probably already settled in her anchorhold and, therefore, would have known of it especially
through those who came to speak about their grief and maybe to
enquire, in desperation, 'how could God let such a tragedy
occur?' Of course she did not have a satisfying answer but she
would most certainly have tried to disabuse them of that all-too-
easily-accepted-thought that suffering is sent to us by God because he wants to punish us for sin. 'If God is love', she would
have said 'he would not, even could not, operate like that'.

There was one other major problem which distressed the
people of that time. It was the spirit of unrest in those who had
for generations been the quiet backbone of the land. For quite a
while the peasants, or the serfs, who had been bound to till the
soil, were dreaming of a world which would be better, more egali-
tarian, a world in which all would indeed be well.[14] Then they
began to organise themselves and to revolt and that of course
began to undermine the very fabric of the medieval way of life.
The feudal Lords reacted as one would expect. Indeed, the Lord

of Norwich, who was also bishop, did so in a most exacting way. Although he was prepared to offer absolution to offenders, he condemned the leaders of the revolution to their death. At such a moment it would not have seemed to those who struggled for a better deal that all things would, or even could, be well, nor did it when the news arrived from London that the Peasants' Rising in that city had been overcome. However, Julian who always had compassion for the suffering, may have helped many of the disillusioned to believe that ultimately all their deepest dreams (if only they could recognise them) would most certainly come true.

We do not know how many people Julian consoled in those disturbing days but she would surely have done all she could to help them find the peace which she herself enjoyed. Moreover, even though we have no more than circumstantial evidence for this, is it not likely that, through helping others, she would have been helped in many ways by them? For instance, by her very listening to what those who came to visit her were saying and by trying to respond to their own special needs, would she not have been helped to see more clearly those particular elements within her own experience which could be relevant to them, in contrast, let us say, to those which may have had a value only for herself? In other words it would have been within a context which contained a dialogue with others that her understanding of God's love and of what it implied would have been both developed and refined. Thus, it would have been with the help of those who came to her for help that she herself was able to become the person that she did: One who was able to enlighten many and to help them on their way.

There was, however, one particular group of people who must surely have assisted Julian in a very special way. I am referring to those theologians who, it seems to me, must have spent many hours in helping her to understand, with fine precision, all the implications of that 'great experience' which was to be so central for whatever words of consolation she might give. Indeed, it may not be too fanciful to think of priestly scholars from a number of the nearby houses of Religious Orders[15] join-

ing the procession to her simple anchorhold. Although they are
not mentioned in her books, it may have been as the result of
their attention and encouragement that she became, first tolerated
by the local church authorities, then more and more accepted as
a person who, while both unclerical and even feminine, was
actually orthodox and, finally, as one who is acknowledged by
the whole church as a guiding light for everyone within a groping
and a searching world.[16] No small achievement that!

However, I remember one participant in a group which I had
just addressed asserting with some vigour that, if Julian had not
been so enclosed, she might have done much more for the de-
prived and suffering people of her time. It was, I felt, a totally
unfair remark. Apart from a presumption that her options in the
fourteenth century were those of our own, it seemed to say that
Julian had not the right, which everyone would claim today, of
following what she considered her own personal vocation. But,
if that in fact is what she did, we can say that, within the context
of her chosen way of life, she made a very valuable and a most
important contribution to the people of her time and through
her books, her influence continues still. Indeed, it could be argued that, if she had not been so enclosed or if she did not have
the opportunity to be alone, she would not have had been able to
contribute all she did.

Notes
1. The anchorhold adjacent to the church of St Julian belonged to the
Benedictine nuns at nearby Carrow. We do not know if Julian had been
a nun of that community or, in some structured way, associated with it.
What is quite certain, and of interest, is that it is due in no small way to
later Benedictine nuns that what she wrote has been preserved for us.
2. cf ST. chapter 9 and LT chapter 15. In neither of these cases was there
any effort made by Julian to quote with accuracy.

3. It was the custom to provide a window or a squint through which an anchoress could see at least the elevated host. That was a most important element in Medieval piety.

4. The window would have been most probably no more than just an opening in the wall and would have been quite small (in order to preserve whatever heat there may have been within) and covered with a cloth (to keep distractions out!). As for the people who consulted Julian herself, the only one we actually know of is the famous Margery Kempe who probably consulted everyone who was reputed to be holy. That itself may be, of course, a testimony to the role which Julian played in the society of her own day. In any case, what she told Margery was wise enough. It was 'to be obedient to the will of our Lord God and fulfil with all her might whatever he put in her soul, if it were not against the worship of God and profit of her even-christians'.

5. Confusion about the actual date was caused by the use of Roman numerals. Thirteen is written as XIII and eight as VIII, a similarity which could and did, apparently, facilitate a scribal error when some manuscript was being copied. However, if the former version is correct a footnote of Grace Warrack is of interest. She wrote 'This must have been a Friday for Easter Sunday of 1373 was on the 17th April'. (This would have been, of course, according to a calendar which has been superseded by the one we use today.)

6. cf. *ST* chapter 10.

7. This gesture was part of the rite prescribed for visiting the dying. cf.*The Stripping of the Altars* by Eamon Duffy, Yale University Press, 1992.

8. cf. *Christ our Mother* by Brant Pelphrey

9. cf. *Life After Life* by Raymond A. Moddy, Bantam Books, 1976.

10. cf. *ST* chapter 1 and *LT* chapter 3

11. Devotion to the human Christ began to grow in the Middle Ages. Sometime later we discover that that same devotion started to become more focused on his Passion. This was due, in no small way, to the Franciscan friars, whose founder was the first to be attributed with having had the stigmata.

12. I have heard of people being conscious of the presence of 'our Lord' when they were dying. I have, moreover, met one lady who described a dream in which a man appeared to beckon her, a man whom she herself identified as Christ. Both situations are, to this extent, the same: they both concern a person who was not controlling his or her own mental process at the time, they both involve some element of psychological projection and in both the 'person-seen' was taken to be Christ.

13. *A Tale of Two Cities* by Charles Dickens (opening paragraph). Note the order given by Dickens was 'the best of times and the worst of times'.

14. John Ball (a priest and leader of the Peasants' Revolt) said in a famous sermon: 'Things cannot go well in England, nor ever shall, till all

be held in common, till there be not bond and free but we are all of one condition.' (cf. 'Contemplative and Radical; Julian meets John Ball', an essay in *Woman of our Day*, Darton, Longman & Todd, London, 1985.)

15. Many of the Religious Orders had a house in Norwich which, at that time, was the second city in the kingdom. Benedictines, Augustinians, Dominicans and Franciscans were all represented there.

16. Julia Holloway argues that Adam Easton, Benedictine and later Cardinal, could have been the influential mentor and protector of Julian. (cf. 'Chronicles of a Mystic', *The Tablet* May 1996)

Part Two

The Mystery of Christ

The crucifix, so central to the spirituality of Julian

By the time that Julian began to write her books she had perceived that her own 'great experience' could be considered as containing 16 different parts, or 'Showings' from the Lord. Of these the first twelve form a certain unity among themselves presenting, as they do, the Christ who suffered and who then was raised up into everlasting life. That was the mystery in which Julian herself participated in a very special way but it is also one which is, she realised, being offered to us all.

The first of these 12 'Showings' could, however, be considered as a kind of overture to all the rest. To say the least, a number of the thoughts which Julian has shared in what she wrote concerning it were taken up and treated by her, often in more detail, later on. I will, however, focus here on only three important points: The central one that God is Love, the complementary one: That our own innate yearnings are for nothing less and, finally, that that love is itself the dynamism of a Trinity which, in the last analysis, involves us even now.

We are concerned with chapters 3-7 in the shorter text and chapters 4-9 in the longer one.

GOD IS LOVE

A platitude?

A thought which does not really fit?

In this connection, let me speak about a fellow-student who was with me many years ago. He would quite frequently appear when some of us were talking in a group and then, not even trying to discover what we were discussing, would quite cheerfully proclaim that: 'God is Love'! We would of course just look at him, at first with some amazement and a laugh, then later with a little irritation since his intervention seemed so totally irrelevant to what was in our minds. Of course, when he had done this many times we tended to ignore him and to keep on talking just as if he were not there at all. But, since I still remember him and his good-humoured efforts to improve us, it is possible that he did have a greater influence on me than I or anybody else could have suspected at the time.

I wonder if the same was true, to some extent at least, for

some of those who listened to the words of Julian herself. Of
course the situation would have been quite different. If they, for
instance, heard her say that 'God is Love', and that was certainly
the essence of her message, it would not have been as members
of a group which was intent on business of its own but as recep-
tive individuals who had decided to approach her for some
badly needed help. But, even so, to hear her say or indicate that
'God is love' may not have always seemed a relevant, or even
likely, answer to the problems which they had. The plague, for
instance, and the war and all the other causes of their sufferings
would have remained and, if they were suggesting anything
about the God who was in charge of everything, it may have
been that he was angry with his people and annoyed.[1] However,
Julian, no more than my once student friend, would not have
tried to push her case and prove that, on the contrary, 'God is
Love'. Yet it would have been obvious to all that she was certain
that he is. Indeed, if some of those who listened to her were not
ready to absorb her insight then, perhaps when they returned to
their own homes her words may have begun, in their own quiet
way, to influence their thinking and their lives.

　　If Julian had thus a part to play in helping others to discover
God's love for themselves, her own conviction had been forged
in her own 'great experience'. But let us note that that particular
and very special moment of awareness may have been made
possible for her by other grace-filled moments in her past.
Indeed, because her writings seem to indicate that, as a person,
she was balanced and secure, we could perhaps conclude that
probably she had been brought up in a loving home and by a
very caring mother.[2] If that was in fact the case, then it would
have been all those early moments in her life, surrounded by her
mother, family and friends, which would have moulded her to
be a person able to accept that very special grace which actually
came to her at thirty-and-a-half. Moreover, those same loving
moments may have given her that confidence in human nature
which enabled her in later life to be a wise and spiritual mother
to all those who looked to her for help. They may have taught
her how to let such people work through many problems, while

continuing to coax them towards the only One who could give them the peace and love which they so much desired.

But let us, as it were, return with some of those who had been listening to her to their homes! It was, perhaps, in that environment that they remembered how she had referred to God as if he were in some way like the very clothes we wear. Indeed, that thought may have reminded them of moments in their own lives when they seemed to have been, as it were, enfolded in the kind of love which Julian appeared to know. They may have even for a while begun to think of God himself in terms which would have been much more maternal than the ones they usually had. In any case, the memory of such consoling moments may have helped them to expect and to receive again that life-infusing grace which Julian was so convinced that God desired them to enjoy.

That thought reminds me of a question which has often come into my mind. It is: did Julian, who spoke of God as One who was enfolding her, attempt at any time to re-enact the kind of situation which had signified for her that vitalising truth? It certainly is easy to imagine her on cold and frosty nights collecting extra blankets or perhaps another shawl and wrapping them around her for a little extra warmth. The question, therefore, ought to be: did she, in doing that, recall at times that moment in her 'great experience' when she was in a very special way enfolded, not just with some ordinary clothes, but with the presence of the loving God himself? Perhaps she did. Perhaps she even pioneered what has become in recent times a worked-out exercise for prayer.[3] In any case her words suggest to those who read them that, within the womb-like comfort of enfolding clothes, we all are able to become aware of One who wants to nourish us with his all-conquering and never-ending life.

He is our clothing, who wraps us and enfolds us for love, embraces us, surrounds us for his love, which is so tender that he may never desert us. (LT 5)

Jerusalem! The mountains surround her, so the Lord surrounds his people, both now and for ever. (Ps 124/125)

You have all clothed yourselves in Christ. (Gal 3:27)

HUMAN WANTING & DESIRE

We want so many things. We always do and, looking back upon our lives, we know we always have. We know, however, that we did not always get what we desired. But we know too that, when we can accept such disappointing facts, we can discover that the very things which we desire are often not as necessary as they sometimes seem to be.

I can recall in this connection one occasion in my early life when I had wanted something very much and was indeed dismayed when I had to accept the fact that it would not be mine. It was no more than just the prize for posting-in the right solution to a crossword puzzle which a Sunday paper used to print but I had wanted that particular prize so very, very much. Indeed I wanted to donate the money to some special and most worthy cause, although I must confess I cannot now remember what it was. At any rate, I prayed each day that I would win and so I was extremely disappointed when, a fortnight later, I did not discover my own name among the lucky ones. It was an almost devastating blow to my sincere, if teen-age, faith. Indeed, it took me quite a while to come to terms with the idea that, in the mind of God, my winning of that crossword puzzle was not so important as it had been in my own.

There must be many people in the world who, at some moment in their lives, have had some similar experience. Indeed, to go back to the days of Julian, there must have been a lot of really needy people then who prayed for graces which they did not get, although those graces could have been much more important for their lives and happiness than was the winning of a crossword puzzle for my own. We could, no doubt, compile a list of their most likely needs but what concerns us here is how those people would, in general, have been assisted at the anchorhold of Julian. Of course we can but guess how she would have consoled or counselled them yet there are certain clues within the pages of her books which seem to say that she responded to three different types of people in three very different ways.

To some of those who came to visit her she may have said no more than 'Yes, of course, you can keep asking God for anything you want.'[4] In that case I would think that she was trying to respond to people who desired some special blessing and were not yet ready to consider any other. But, if Julian was able to accept them as they were, the evidence is that she would have spoken to them in a way which would have left them free to find that deeper part within themselves which needed something else. In other words, she would have intimated that the God from whom her visitors were hoping to receive what they desired is One who is all-love and so much more important and desirable than any secondary gift. Such was the way that Julian herself regarded God and she, it seems to me, was very sure that anyone who could approach him in that spirit would eventually sense within themselves that deeper need, which is of course within us all, and which He certainly desires to answer and fulfil.

However, with a second type of visitor it might have been much easier for Julian to say a little more. Indeed, it might have been, not only possible, but opportune to speak about this deeper need and that, it seems to me, is what she must have often done. I have in mind one sentence in her second book in which she makes a reference to what she calls our 'natural will for God' and indicates how strong and how persistent it can be. Perhaps the term, 'the natural will' is not the best because it might suggest, and does to some, that it is something which can bring us almost painlessly to God without deliberate choosing on our part, or without any help from him. But Julian, of course, did not mean that, as we will have an opportunity to note. She only wanted to allow her visitors, and future readers, to accept and to enjoy that innate yearning for the Infinite which is within us all and cannot be for very long ignored.

But here, perhaps, we ought to let her speak about her famous hazel nut.

It was within her 'great experience' that Julian had seen this tiny thing which was, she tells us, lying in the hollow of her hand. It was, indeed, so very small and, as she contemplated it, the thought seems to have come into her mind that, if it were to fall, it could so easily just roll away and be completely lost! But, then, she realised that all creation in the hand of God is also very small and that, if he did not continue loving it with care, it too would disappear. However, as she shared that insight with some visitors in later life, she may have often left it to themselves to find and to accept the message it contained. She, therefore, may have only smiled, aware that they were even then beginning to perceive the salutary fact: that all those many things which this world can provide are also very small and, in the end, unsatisfying when compared with him who, taking care of everything, can fill us with an everlasting life.

There is one other type of person who could have consulted Julian and who deserves a special mention here. It is the one who has, not only found, but also been attuned to this deep, fundamental yearning yet who also finds that he or she is still distracted by so many secondary things. I am quite sure that Julian would have been sympathetic to that kind of person since, to some extent, she too was conscious of those vain affections[5] which can hold us back and keep us from the One who offers all. However, at this point within her second and her longer book, she offers us a prayer which obviously meant a lot to her and which some of her friends may have found very useful too. It reads:

God of your goodness give me yourself ...
If I ask for what is less, I will not have enough.
Only in you do I have everything.

Perhaps, in writing it, she felt that maybe some of her own future readers would discover that it is, indeed, the kind of prayer which can, not only keep our fundamental yearning focused, but enlivened too.

We may with reverence ask from our Lover all that we will. (*LT* 6)

The Father who is in heaven knows how to give good things to those who ask him. (Mt 7:11)

He showed me something small no bigger than a hazel nut, lying in the palm of my hand... I thought, because of its littleness, it would suddenly have fallen into nothing. (*LT* 5)

Behold the nations are like a drop from a bucket, and are accounted as the dust on the scales. (Is 40:15)

This is the reason why our hearts and souls are not in perfect ease, because here we seek rest in this thing which is so little, in which there is no rest. (*LT* 5)

Do not set your heart on riches, even when they increase. (Ps 61/62)

Our natural will is to have God, and God's good will is to have us and we can never stop willing or loving until we possess him in the fullness of joy. (LT 6)

Apart from you I want nothing on earth...

My body and my heart faint for joy; God is my possession forever. (Ps 72/73)

God, of your goodness, give me yourself. (LT 5)

O God, you are my God, for you I long. (Ps 62/63)

THE TRINITY IS UNDERSTOOD

The Trinity is a mystery. Of course! Indeed it would be rather strange if we, who often find it difficult to understand another human being, were to comprehend what is no other than the hidden life of the transcendent God. There was good reason, therefore, for a certain parish priest to be surprised when someone, who had been attending lectures I was giving on the topic of the Trinity declared: 'I understand it now'! However, even if she didn't (and that was of course the case), that does not mean that it does not have any value for our lives.

However, let us stay with Julian, our spiritual guide. She spoke, in her own way, about the 'Trinity' and much of what she said was surely influenced by teaching which she had received and by the prayers which, as an anchoress, she would have said each day. However, when I came across her statement that 'Where Jesus appears the Blessed Trinity is understood',[6] I was surprised and wondered what she could have meant. The Blessed Trinity, according to accepted Christian teaching, is three Persons, Father, Son and Holy Spirit and, while Julian was not suggesting that one could be three, I still had to discover how she could have come to think of Jesus as a person who was indicating all. The only way to do so was of course to read right though her second book, the one in which this statement had been made, and hope, that as I did, I would discover other statements which would indicate what this preliminary one implied.

But let us first go back to Julian's own 'great experience' which happened when she saw the crucifix which had been held before her as she lay so sick in bed.[7] We know that as she looked at it, she was aware of being loved and that she realised that he, whom she saw on the cross, was manifesting that love to her in a very special way. Of course she would have known that he, according to accepted Christian teaching, was divine and she did not have any problem in accepting that. However, let us not too quickly make that mental jump which says 'divinity means Trinity' because, although that also was the teaching of the church, it is a thought which Julian had not yet thought through at the time. But, on the other hand, what might be interesting to note is that within her 'great experience' there was at least (although she did not formulate it in this way) a 'kind of trinity' at work: there was in other words the One whom Julian perceived, there was herself responding and, although it was not named, there was a spirit bringing them together into one.

As Julian herself reflected later on that 'great experience' of hers she came to see that Jesus had been, not just loving her, but also manifesting someone else. But here again her analysing and absorbing mind was being influenced by the official and accepted teaching of the church. It had declared, from very early times, that all who see the Son are able to perceive the Father too.[8] Thus Julian herself was able to declare in her own pithy way: 'I saw in Christ that the Father is.'[9] But, what concerns us here is not so much that she began to think of Jesus as the filial expression of the Father but that she was one who, while retaining her own personal devotion to the crucified, was able to perceive that personal devotion in a context which was greater than itself. That context was that of a network of relationships, that of the Father with the Son, that of the Father with herself and that of her involvement in the spirit which made all of them as one. Moreover, and this should be underlined, it was because she could do that that her own thoughts became of value, not just to herself or to a certain few, but to her 'even-christians' everywhere.

Apart from grace, what seems to have caused Julian to move in this direction was her own persistent efforts to perceive the meaning of an unexpected picture-parable which was within her 'great experience'.[10] In brief, that picture-parable portrayed a person who had both the dress and the appearance of a servant, though he seemed to be a servant who was more than usually willing to obey his noble lord. Indeed, so willing was he that, in his attempt to do his best, he fell into a ditch from which he could not rise. 'Who was he?', wondered Julian. He seemed to her to be too good to symbolise all humankind which might have been the case had his appearance in her 'great experience' been just the consequence of some remembered medieval mystery play. However, after she had struggled with this picture-parable for quite a while, (indeed for up to twenty years) some other thoughts which helped her came into her mind. One was that 'humankind' should be considered as including Christ; another that it could be thought of as personified by him. In consequence, the good and noble servant in the picture-parable could be in fact interpreted as symbolising humankind both in its greatness, as revealed in Christ, and in its struggles and distress, which are so obviously in us all.

We will be able, in a later chapter, to examine other aspects of this picture-parable but now it may be of some value just to underline the necessary changes in perspective which it caused. The first concerned the role of Christ himself. He had been just the one whom Julian perceived as loving her, the one whom she acknowledged as her Lord and to whom she had such a deep and personal devotion. But, as a result of what her picture-parable revealed, she came to see him in relation to another person too. It was at this stage that the teaching of the church came to her aid again. It spoke of Christ as one who came to serve but also of the One who sent him and whose will it was his great desire to do. Thus once again for Julian a trinitarian design began to show: there was the Servant-Christ, there was the Father-Lord, and, once again, there was a spirit which, although it was not mentioned, was the bond which made them one.

The consequence of this new understanding was important. Since the Servant was, not only Christ considered as an individual, but Christ as everyone, the visitors who came to Julian (and everybody else) had also to be thought of in the context of this trinitarian design. For Julian to minister to them was, therefore, more than just an overflow of her own life with Christ. It was the consequence of knowing that in some way she already was united with them and that they, although perhaps in different ways, were being influenced by that same spirit which was animating her. Thus there emerged, not just 'a kind of trinity' (as we have seen above), but an extension of that Blessed Trinity which was so prominent within the teaching of the church. It was that Trinity of Christ, including everyone, and of the Spirit which can bring us more and more into his life and of the everlasting Father who is lovingly accepting all.

In consequence, the Trinity for Julian was not some total mystery which was separated from her ordinary life. It was that very life in which both she and everybody were involved. It was a dynamism of transcendent love which could and would enhance all human nature as it was embraced. Of course it must be said again that her experiences did not prove that such a Blessed Trinity exists. But, on the other hand, once its existence is accepted as a reasonable article of faith, experiences (be they Julian's or ours) can make it seem, not only relevant, but also as a marvellous and unifying life to which we all have reason to aspire.

Our good Lord revealed to me that it is greatly pleasing to him that a simple soul should come naked, openly and familiarly. For this is the loving yearning of the soul through the touch of the Holy Spirit. (LT 51)

I am my beloved's and his desire is for me. (Cant 7:10)

The Lord is God the Father, the servant is the Son, Jesus Christ. The Holy Spirit is the equal love which is within them both. (LT 51)

When Jesus was praying the Holy Spirit descended upon him as a dove and a voice came from heaven, saying: 'This is my beloved Son.' (Lk 3:21-22)

I understood that the servant who stood before him (i.e. before the Lord) was Adam for in the sight of God all men are one man and one man is all ... Now the Son does not stand before the Father as a servant ... but richly clothed ... with a precious crown upon his head. We are his crown, which crown is the Father's joy, the Son's honour, the Holy Spirit's delight. (LT1)

The grace of our Lord Jesus Christ and the love of God and the fellowship of the Holy Spirit be with you all. (2 Cor 13:14)

Notes.

1. Disasters were quite easily associated with divine activity. They could be thought of as the 'remedies' which God provides to change our ways. However, words like 'punishments' (instead of 'remedies') and 'wrath' in God (instead of 'healing power') could easily suggest a deity which would be very much at variance with the loving One of Julian. It could be noted that the tendency to think of such disasters as the punishments which have been sent by an angry God emerged in even very recent times with the appearance and the spread of AIDS.

2. The only reference to Julian's mother is found in the Short Text where she is described as putting out her hand to close the eyes of her daughter when it seemed that she had died. (cf. ST chapter 10). This detail, like all others which could be considered personal, is not found in the Longer Text.

3. Anthony de Mello offered this as an 'awareness exercise'. He told the readers of his book to let themselves 'become aware of the touch of clothes on... shoulders, back' and every other part of their own bodies. Such awareness will, he tells them, bring them to the present moment which of course is where God can be found. (cf *Sadhana*, Gujarat Sahitya Prakash Anand, India)

4. 'We may with reverence ask from our lover all that we want' (cf. LT chapter 6)

5. cf. ST chapter 13 & LT chapter 27

6. cf. LT chapter 4.

7. cf. ST chapter 2 & LT chapter 3.

8. cf. Jn 14:9.

9. cf. LT chapter 22. Julian did not try to develop any Trinitarian theology but it, the Trinity,was presupposed in everything she said. Some thoughts which could be traced back to the works of other writers can be found but her own presentation was essentially her own.

10. cf. LT. chapter 51. This long chapter contains the picture-parable and the meaning which was seen in it, eventually, by Julian.

Five 'Showings' are our subject now, (the 2nd, 3rd, 4th, 5th and 6th).
They could be thought of as a group among themselves, at least to the
extent that they were all preliminary to the great climactic ones in
which the dying of the crucified and something of the joy of his new life
were shown. These five, however, were, like all the other ones which
Julian received, related to the essence of her 'great experience', which
was of being loved as she had never been before. Thus while some im-
ages of Christ, the crucifed, impinged themselves upon her conscious
mind from time to time they did so as expressions of that all-surpassing
love. (cf. 2nd & 4th 'Showings'.) Julian, however, was aware that the
divinity itself is somehow everywhere (cf. 3rd 'Showing') and that,
through Christ, it is forever offering a life which can fill all of us with
joy and even wholesome mirth (cf. 5th & 6th 'Showings').

We are concerned with some of chapter seven in the Short Text,
then with chapter eight and part of chapter nine. In the Long Text, all
these 'Showings' are in chapters ten until fourteen, inclusively.

OFFERED GIFTS

Julian, when speaking of the message of her second Showing,
underlined some gifts which God desires to give.

That second 'Showing' had been rather strange. Indeed, for
quite some time it seems that Julian herself was not too sure that
it was one at all. She, certainly, was sure that she continued seeing Christ as he was in his passion and that for a while the clarity
of what she saw was poor. That could, of course, have been because her sight was failing, which was possible as she was at
that moment very close to death. It also could have been because
the room itself was dark, which would have been the case since
it was in the middle of the night.[1] But, while there may have
been some measurable reason for not seeing all that she desired,
this 'seeing yet not-seeing' episode continued to intrigue her.
She kept on returning to it in the years ahead, especially perhaps
when she had come to the conclusion that it was in fact a
'Showing' in itself and one which had a separate and most important message of its own.[2]

This episode in fact had made her conscious of the great desire within herself to see more than she did. However, at the time, she had been soothed by the thought that, if God wanted her to see more clearly or indeed if it was necessary for her that she should, then he would give her all the light that she required. So, was the message of this Showing that she could and should relax although she did not see as much as she herself desired? Perhaps it was. Indeed, it seems that Julian accepted that it was and that she would say afterwards to people who were so submerged in their own troubles that they felt that they were drowning that they too could find a reason to relax. (Her image of being at the bottom of the sea may have been influenced by tales of maritime disasters told by sea-folk who would have frequented her adjacent church.[3] However it may also have been sparked off by the verses of a psalm she knew.[4]) In any case, what most concerns us here is just the fact that Julian herself became much more convinced that, even though what we can see within the light of faith seems very indistinct, it still can be sufficient for the guidance of our lives.

As Julian continued to reflect on this 'not-seeing and yet seeing' episode and to discuss some aspects of it with her evenchristians, she began to realise that it suggested certain gifts which God desires to give us for our use until our own desire to see him is completely satisfied. The first is that of seeking him but with a careful diligence and balanced by the second, complementary gift of waiting patiently when he cannot be found.

The first, that is 'to seek God diligently', seems to indicate that we must make some effort in our search. For Julian herself that obviously meant, apart from other things, the prayerful pondering of her own 'great experience' which had been so important for her life. But, since she must have pondered it within the context of the scriptures and the whole tradition of the church, as we have seen, her 'diligence' must have involved a relatively constant mental exercise throughout a large part of her life. No doubt it also meant excluding thoughts which could distract her from her purpose or, if she decided to accept them, making sure that they were placed within the context of her more important ones. Like someone who was furnishing a room, it seems that Julian did all she could to furnish her own mind with a variety of valuable thoughts among which she would then be able to relax and quietly allow her spirit to be free.

As for that gift of 'waiting patiently' or, as she put it, 'without grumbling', it suggests a calm acceptance of the difficult events of life together with the certainty that, like the vision in her second 'Showing', they contain a meaning and a purpose which may only in the future be revealed. For Julian that kind of waiting must have meant accepting with as positive an attitude as possible, not only major tragedies such as the plague but all the minor inconveniences of life as well. These latter may have been for her no more than the arrival of some person at an inconvenient hour or with an attitude which, for some reason, could succeed in irritating her. Indeed, in this connection it may be of interest to observe that earlier in this same chapter of her book she had referred to 'suffering', instead of 'waiting', and a few lines later of 'surrendering' to God. It was as if she recognised that 'suffering' the unavoidable annoyances that come with life and then 'surrendering' to him whose will they seem to represent were often necessary stages to obtaining that more perfect gift of 'waiting without grumbling' which she knew God certainly desired to give.

There was, however, one more gift which Julian decided should be added to her list. It was the power to trust. Perhaps she added it because her later interest in the Trinity encouraged her to think in threes but, even if that was an influential factor, trusting had for her a value of its own. It was the opposite to doubting and, within her own relationship with God, to doubting that he would in fact some day reveal himself completely and give her the life which she desired. However, while at times she may have wondered if, among the problems of each day, her own trust in his goodness was as strong as it should be, there may have been a lot of people whom she knew who had much less conviction and whom she desired to help. It, consequently, would have been for them as well as for herself that she referred to trust as something which, if hard to do, is ultimately one of those three gifts which God desires to give.Indeed, to keep a little closer to her thought, it was one part of that three-petalled gift of seeking, waiting and of trusting which God wants us all to ask for and to have.

I saw him and I sought him and I had him and I lacked him; and this is and should be our ordinary undertaking in this life, as I see it. (LT 10)

I sought him, whom my soul loves; I sought him but found him not. (Cant 3:1)

The first (gift) is that we seek willingly and dilligently without sloth ... the second (gift) is that we wait for him steadfastly, out of love for him, without grumbling or contending against him, to the end of our lives, for that will last only for a time... The third (gift) is that we have great trust in him, out of complete and true faith, for it is his will that we know that he will appear, suddenly and blessedly, to all his lovers. (LT 10)

Seek first the kingdom of God and his righteousness (Mt 6:33)

Surely, I am coming soon. (Rev 22:20)

Faith is the assurance of things hoped for, the conviction of things not seen. (Heb 11:1)

SIN IS NO DEED

Julian saw God 'in a point'
This is a strange and not-too-easily-interpreted remark. Some people think that what she meant was that she saw him in an instant. Others are inclined to think that it was in some kind of spacial way which was extremely small, though at the same time able to expand and to include all that exists as well.[5] In either case, or in a mixture of the two, this insight may have been a

pleasant and relaxing one, especially because she had felt so
frustrated by not seeing Christ as clearly as she had desired. She
now was brought beyond the seen and not seen physical expressions of his human nature, and indeed beyond that very nature,
and made suddenly aware of life itself in its ubiquitous simplicity.

It was when Julian became aware of God's all-permeating
presence that she noticed an extraordinary fact. It was that there
was no room left for sin. Of course a lot of people whom she
knew would have referred to sin as if it were some verifiable reality and their perception of it was a practical and very valid one
indeed. It was, moreover, one which Julian herself was ready to
accept and in another place she would discuss what it implied.
However, for the moment what impressed, and even startled,
her was that extraordinary fact that, since God is in everything
and since all that exists depends on him, there is no room for
anything which is not God or contrary to his designs. In other
words there is no room for sin and so it is, to use her own expression here, 'no thing'.[6] That insight must have really fascinated
her because, while she could recognise sin's very real and often
quite oppressive presence, she refused to let go of that rarer
point of view which was, not only equally persuasive, but exciting and emancipating too.

It may say something about Julian herself that she was able to
consider sin as nothing and, in spite of all the problems of her
age, to hold on to that much more optimistic point of view. It
may, for instance, indicate that she was one of those who are inclined by temperament, as well as by their personal experience
of life, to see the good which is in everything and so to overlook
the limitations which inevitably everything contains. Of course,
the same may not have been the case for many of the people
whom she knew. A number of them would, no doubt have been
inclined by their own temperament, as well as by the disappointments which they had experienced, to see the not-so-good
in everything and in all people too. Such people find it difficult
to let the deepest level in themselves perceive a guiding and a
loving deity at work in all the situations of their lives and so to

be informed that sin is really nothing may at times have been the
message which they needed most. It may have made it possible
for them to take on board its necessary consequence: that, if all
things are ultimately done by God, all that is done is ultimately
done as well as it can be.

God is everything that is
good, as I see, and the goodness which everything has is
God. (LT 8)

The Spirit of the Lord, indeed, fills the whole world.
(Wis 1:7)

I was compelled to admit that
everything which is done is
done well, for God does
everything... I was certain
that he does no sin and here I
was certain that sin is no
deed (ST 'no thing'). (LT 11)

God did not make death...
(Wis 1:13)

They were astonished be-
yond measure, saying: 'He
has done all things well'.
(Mk 7:37)

A man regards some things
as well done and some as evil
and our Lord does not regard
them so. (LT 11)

Man looks on the outward
appearance but the Lord
looks on the heart.
(1 Sam 16:7)

We do not fail in the sight of
God and we do not stand in
our own sight; and both of
these are true, as I see it but
the way that God sees is the
higher truth. (LT 82)

As the heavens are higher
than the earth, so are my
ways higher than your ways
and my thoughts than your
thoughts. (Is 55:9)

God revealed all this, as
though to say: 'See, I am
God. See, I do all things.' I
saw truly that I must agree
with great reverence and joy.
(LT 11)

Then Job answered the
Lord: I know that you can
do all things, and that no
purpose of yours can be
thwarted. (Job 42:1)

BEING CLEANSED

To know God is to know oneself. To know God's goodness is to realise the goodness which is in oneself. That was an underlying thought of Julian but for the moment what she seems to offer is an intermediary stage. That is when we admire God's goodness and his love for us and then become aware of just how little we deserve it. That, in its own way, was what was happening in the case of one young lady whom I met in Africa. She felt, she told me, so unworthy of her boy-friend whom she recognised as loving her so much! However, she was happy too. Awareness of her failings did not lead her to despair. Nor did it in the case of Julian whose lover was none other than the God who is himself all-love. Indeed it was her own conviction of his never-failing love which made her realise, not only that she was acceptable to him, but that his love would change her more and more.

It was, as if to illustrate this hidden process that some images appeared within her mind. The first one was of water and of being washed. That was, perhaps, a normal and indeed predictable expression of a process which would have included the removing of the stain of any sin. Indeed, when Julian was growing up, she would no doubt have frequently seen clothes being washed in water and made clean by her own mother and by other women of the place. However, in her vision water-washing quickly turned to one which was being done with blood. That was not something which she would have seen at home but it bears witness to another major source, that of the sacred scriptures, which had influenced her way of thinking and her life. It was, no doubt, through preachers that she would have heard about the blood of Christ, or of the Lamb, in which all sin is washed away. Perhaps she may have even read translations of such scripture passages when she was living in her anchorhold.[7] In any case, she had no problem in accepting such a vivid image as a symbol of the life of Christ as his own love surrounded her and cleansed her to become like him who is himself the perfect image of the Father's overflowing love.

As Julian continued to reflect on this part of her 'great experience' she came to see more clearly its importance, not just for herself, but also for the people whom she knew. The life which flowed from Christ was seen by her to be for humankind itself. It was for all who were alive while she was writing and for all who had already died and also for those people who, at that time, had not yet been born. But let us note again that sense of careful caution which she had. She was prepared to speak of those 'who are, have been or will be of good will' without declaring whether such a group included everyone or not. However, she herself was open to the wider possibility and happily insisted that the blood of Christ was plentiful enough to heal and save all those whom God in his great love had made. That was enough! It, certainly, was quite sufficient to encourage her to love her 'even-christians' and to give herself to those who, conscious of their own unworthiness, came to her anchorhold for help.

There is, however, one remark of Julian which seems to beg for some interpretation here. It is the one which says that, when the blood of Christ which she saw flowing from his wounds fell to the ground, 'it disappeared'. That unexpected comment could have meant that, at a certain time, the blood would have accomplished all that it was shed to do. In other words, all people of goodwill will have, by then, been saved and consequently healing will have been complete. But, it could also be interpreted as meaning that the healing which we need in this life can continue to take place although it is not seen. This second possibility can claim support from Julian's admitted fact that her extraordinary visions ceased, implying that whatever healing she still needed in this life would happen in the dimness of the light of ordinary faith. If this is what she meant, it might be useful to associate this disappearance of the healing blood with her suggestion that we should allow the very memory of sin to disappear as well.[8] Indeed, if God sees in us only what is good, should we not try to do the same, and so facilitate the unseen healing action of his presence in our lives?

It came to my mind that God has created bountiful water on the earth for our use and our bodily comfort out of the tender love he has for us. (LT 12)

O purify me,
then I shall be clean;
O wash me,
I shall be whiter than snow.
(Ps 50/51)

It is more pleasing to him that we accept for our total cure his blessed blood to wash us of our sins. (LT 12)

'Drink of it all of you; for this is the blood of the covenant, which is poured out for many for the forgiveness of sins'. (Mt 26:27-28)

The precious plenty of his precious blood overflows all the earth and it is ready to wash from their sins all creatures who are, have been and will be of good will. (LT 12)

To him who loves us and has freed us from our sins by his blood, to him be glory and dominion for ever and ever, Amen. (Rev 1:5-6)

As it, the blood, flowed down to where it should have fallen, it disappeared. (LT 12)

Blessed are those who have not yet seen and yet believe. (Jn 20:29)

LAUGHTER

Julian laughed and, when she did, all those who were around her laughed as well.

She laughed because she suddenly felt very, very free. The sense of being stained by sin which had affected her was, for the moment, gone. Life, therefore, seemed to flow within her once again and she, relieved and taken somewhat by surprise, allowed it to express itself in that spontaneous and unexpected laugh. It was a laugh which was contagious too, as those who were around her bed discovered for themselves. But laughter can quite often be like that.

A long tradition had disparaged laughter since it often is at

somebody's expense.[9] But, if there was an element of mockery
in Julian when she laughed, it was not aimed at any other
human being but at one who has personified all evil for so many
people down the ages and whom she herself referred to as the
fiend.[10] Since that older English word, which meant an evil spirit,
was synonymous in this case with the devil, it may be of interest
here to note an exclamation of that nineteenth-century Bishop,
William Ullathorne. When on his deathbed he heard someone
pray that he might be preserved from all the devil's snares, he
interjected with those memorable words: 'the devil is an ass!'[11]
Although he may not have been conscious of it at the time, he
was, in saying that, a follower of Julian and his disdain for that
arch-enemy can be, as is her own, a healthy antidote for all of us
if thinking of the devil makes us feel uneasy and, perhaps, a little insecure. As Julian knew well, it can be good to laugh. Indeed
it is important to enjoy the comforting which good and non-con-
taminated laughter can provide.

Perhaps the people who had come around the dying Julian
began to laugh because they thought her laughing was a sign
that she might live. However, what may be of special interest to
us here is, not that they perceived a gleam of hope, but that their
laughter brought some further happiness to Julian herself.
Indeed, when she referred to laughter in her second book, she
did so in a way which indicates, not only that she liked to laugh,
but also that she realised its value for the spreading of the good
news which she wanted to achieve.

She may at first, if I may speculate, have come to realise that
her own pleasure at the laughter of those people who had come
around her bed was not unlike the pleasure which she may have
had in later life when others, who had come to her weighed
down with problems, found that they could do the same.
However (and I speculate again) she then may have begun to realise that, having listened to their woes, it could at times be useful to them if, instead of just suggesting that there was a deeper
level in themselves where they could still be free, she could express her own delight at having found it for herself. Not only

could such buoyancy encourage those who were oppressed with problems to relax but it could also offer them a sign of hope which might in turn help them to find true freedom for themselves. If that is what occurred when people came to Julian, and I suspect it often was, her fundamental cheerfulness may well have been her most important contribution to the welfare of their lives. We are not told how much she was appreciated for this at the time but she deserves from us at least a word of gratitude for that all-too-infrequent testimony to the benefit of pure and happy laughter which she gave.

I understood that we may laugh, to comfort ourselves and rejoice in God, because the devil is overcome. (LT 13)

When the Lord delivered Zion from bondage, it seemed like a dream. Then was our mouth filled with laughter, on our lips there were songs. (Ps 125/126)

BEING THANKED

After the laughter there was joy. Indeed, it seems that at this moment in her 'great experience' the joy of Julian was very great indeed. She felt that she was totally accepted, honoured, even praised and that was truly wonderful. Moreover, when she tried to analyse that special moment in the days ahead (that is before she had begun to write) she noticed that her joy had been composed of, not just one, but three exciting elements. The first was that the God of all was thanking her, despite the fact that she was just 'a sinful creature'[12] who had not done very much. The second was that he was doing this in public and the third that all the love and honour which she was receiving would continue without end.

As Julian reflected on that unexpected moment of exceeding joy and tried to speak of it to others, she began to understand it in connection with some images which came into her mind. They were concerned with kings and banquets and the giving of great honours, all of which would have been part of courtly life

in Norwich at the time. Was it not, then, the second most important city in the kingdom? But, while her own images were thus,
to some extent, in harmony with her society, the influence of
gospel parables is evident in them as well. One is, indeed, reminded of the well-known parable which spoke about a king
who gave a very splendid banquet for his son.[13]

However, there were some important details in these images
of Julian which may have been spontaneous expressions of herself. For instance, there was that great courtesy and friendliness
which she saw in the king. There was, in consequence, the way
that he appeared to fill the very place in which he lived with
happiness and joy and, finally, there was the happy fact that all
who came to him were thereby able to behave as if they were his
very special and important friends. If all those details were in
some way illustrating Julian's own friendly personality, the
sharing of them may have helped a number of her visitors to be
much more relaxed in their relationship with God and, consequently, much less apprehensive about meeting him on
Judgement day. Indeed, those images could have encouraged
them to think of God, not as a cold and calculating judge as
many did, but as a loving One who will appreciate the good
which is in each and in whose radiating presence they and
everybody will delight to be.

Julian herself, as she reflected on this moment of her 'great
experience', appears to have found special pleasure in the fact
that in the second of her images there were so many people who
could see the honour which the king was giving to each one.
Perhaps her interest in that detail came from some need in herself for public recognition which she thought she was not get-
ting at the time.[14] However it could also have been caused by
knowing that she was in fact appreciated and that in the world
to come that good experience would have to be, not just repeated,
but most wonderfully magnified. In either case the thought of
others being with us when we are received by God can make
that moment even more enticing than it otherwise might be.
Instead of entering into a spiritual but unsocial state we will, so

Julian assures us, have the company of many friends whom God will be forever filling with his joy and, if I may use her appealing word, his everlasting 'mirth'.[15]

As we consider this short chapter in the longer book of Julian, we may begin to see a certain pattern emerge. It is that of the Trinity itself. In fact a lot of what she came to say about this showing was the consequence of her belated understanding of that picture-parable about the servant and the lord.[16] Thus, as the lord in that thought-changing parable was finally perceived to be the Father, so too was the person of the King in these two images which are our subject here. In consequence the servant in the picture-parable and the recipient of gratitude and honour in these images were, not just Julian herself, nor anyone of her own fellowmen or women in this world, but Christ himself that 'one man'[17] who includes us all. It, consequently, is with him (and in the Spirit) that each one of us will be enabled to receive the 'honourable thanks' which he so much deserves and which the loving Father wants so lovingly to give.

But Julian decided to conclude this section in her second book with what might be considered as a moralising afterthought. It is that thinking about God as one who wants to do so much for us can make us more disposed to do his will each day. Indeed she clearly states that as we contemplate his loving courtesy our willingness to serve him can increase. No doubt she spoke from her own personal experience which would have come, not just from moments when to do his will was relatively easy, but from those when it was difficult as well. Her message to her readers here, however, seems to be that they should keep their focus on the One who loves them and whose gratitude, when manifested, will be always sheer surprise.[18]

I saw him reign in his house as a king and fill it full of joy and mirth, gladdening and consoling his dear friends with himself. (LT 14)

The kingdom of heaven can be compared to a king who gave a marriage feast for his son. (Mt 22:2)

If a king thank his subjects, it is a great honour for them; and if he makes this known to all his kingdom, then their honour is much increased. (LT 14)

Then the king will say to those at his right hand: 'Come, inherit the kingdom prepared for you'. (Mt 25:34)

The honourable thanks that one man will have, who has voluntarily served God. (LT 14)

Truly, truly, I say to you, he will gird himself and have them sit at table and he will come and serve them. (Lk:12:37)

Notes

1. cf. ST. chapter 2 & LT. chapter 3.

2. Julian was conscious of the difference between a 'bodily vision' and a 'spiritual one'. She was aware, moreover, that a bodily vision was, not only less important than a spiritual one, but that it was not even necessary for our growth.

3. The church adjacent to the anchorhold of Julian was dedicated to St Julian, presumably the patron saint of ferrymen. It could be noted that the river Wensum, which in those days could be navigated up to Norwich, was quite near. Moreover, it is reasonable to suppose that, not just ferrymen, but also sea-folk from the ships which had been moored not far away, would have come to St Julian's for Mass and other services.

4. cf. 'Save me, O Lord, for the waters have risen to my neck, I have entered the waters of the deep and the waters overwhelm me' (Ps 68/69)

5. It is possible, as many commentators think, that Julian had in mind a knitting-stitch. It could have been imagined by her as developing and

spreading out to make and to include the total article as each part started to exist.

6. Julian follows here a way of thinking which could be considered Augustinian. However, it could be associated too with one Old Testament idea of sin, that of a 'falling short' of what was meant to be.

7. Some translations of the scriptures were available in those days but many of them were associated with the Lollards and a person using them could, therefore, be considered suspect of those peoples's unacceptable beliefs. They were a group who, while demanding clerical reform, would not accept ecclesiastical authority, a fact which did not make them popular nor did it help their cause. Indeed, in 1397 a group of bishops, including Henry Despenser of Norwich, asked for and obtained permission to condemn convicted Lollards to the stake. The execution place in Norwich was near the present railway station and within a smelling-distance of the anchorhold of Julian!

8. cf. 'God forgets our sins just so he wishes us to forget our sins' (LT. chapter 73) Consequently it may not be always of much use 'to call to mind our sins'. Indeed, if one is able to forget them, it may mean that healing has already taken place.

9. Even the scriptures spoke of laughter in a deprecatory way. If it was not considered as a form of mockery (cf. Mk 5:40) it was often understood as incompatible with this preparatory life (cf. Lk 6: 25). However there were some occasions when a laughter which was good and even celebratory received a passing mention. (cf. Ps 125/126 above and Job 8:21)

10. Julian spoke about the devil (or the fiend) in her books. In doing so she was but following the ordinary teaching of the church. However, it is arguable that the concept of a being who is damned for all eternity fits awkwardly into her basic intuition of a God who is all-love and who will, consequently, make all to be well.

11. cf. *The Life and Times of Bishop Ullathorne* by Cuthbert Butler, Vol. 2, p. 295. Burns Oates & Washbourne Ltd, 1926.

12. cf. LT chapter 4.

13. cf. Mt 22:1ff

14. cf. LT chapter 28.

15. According to the teaching of the church, a General Judgement will take place at the end of time when everyone will come before the judgement seat of God. It is distinguised from the personal or particular judgement when each individual at his or her own death will get the sentence he or she deserves. Julian, however, did not use such terms. Indeed she seems to see the two events as one and, certainly, she has described that great climactic moment for us in a most appealing way

16. cf. LT chapter 51.

17. 'It seemed to me that all the pain and labour which all living men might endure could not earn the honourable thanks that one man will have who was voluntarily served God' (LT 14) The 'one man' would seem to have been the inclusive Christ.

18. In the Long Text Julian tells us that 'her understanding was lifted up' which seems to indicate a sudden and extraordinary insight.

We now come to the great climactic moment of this mystery in which Julian became so totally involved. It was that of the dying and the rising to a new and everlasting life of Christ.

We will, however, focus on the dying aspect of the mystery first and so on both the 7th and the 8th of Julian's enumerated 'Showings'.

We will, consequently, be concerned with that part of the Short Text which begins half way through chapter 9 and then continues until the end of the 11th and, within the longer text, with six whole chapters: 15 until 20.

In Woe and in Weal

After being happy, Julian was sad. Then once again her happiness returned but only to give way to yet another period in which she felt depressed. Such moods continued to replace each other for a while and, as they did, they formed the background for what she would come to recognise as both a new and very valuable message. It was that, while human beings often change, God always stays the same. That was, of course not something which she did not know before but at that very moment it became a stabilising fact which, in the midst of constant change, gave her both confidence and hope.

The alternating pattern which Julian observed within her 'great experience' may have appeared to her in retrospect like an intensified, if relatively short, example of the ups and downs which she was to experience throughout her later life. The weariness, for instance, which she felt within her 'great experience' may have been seen in later life, and even understood to some extent, through the experience of other weary moments which she was to have. Indeed, there must have been occasions when, within the isolation of her anchorhold, she felt 'fed up', abandoned by the flow of life and, therefore, very much alone. Did she not in a later chapter of her longer book admit that where she lived seemed sometimes like a prison from which part of her would have been willing to escape?[1] However, Julian did not elaborate on such depressing moments as she wrote and it is most unlikely that she would have even spoken of them to her ordinary guests. She was too much convinced about the value of her better moments and of all that they implied.

As Julian reflected on the ups and downs which come in life she came to see, with sadness, that some people do not profit from them in the way that she felt that they should.[2] Of course, she was aware that often 'feeling down' could be, to some extent at least, the consequence of something which those very people had or had not done. In that case she, no doubt, would have encouraged them to find the underlying cause of their distress and, then, to do whatever was required?[3] But Julian was also very conscious that there are occasions when this 'feeling down' is caused by circumstances over which the sufferer has really no control at all. In such a situation she would probably have done her best to stop her anguished visitor from being too preoccupied with his or her own physical or mental pain. Indeed, she may have even intimated that, while he or she felt weak and powerless in a sea of many troubles, there was One not very far away who could and would extend to them, as he had often done to her, a helping and a saving hand.[4]

The central message which this 'Showing' offered and which Julian desired to share was, therefore, that in times of sorrow as of joy we have good reason to believe that God does not withdraw his saving care. The way that she herself proclaimed that good news through her books was that 'in woe and weal', or 'weal and woe', God always keeps us safe. Those words, of course, come from an older form of English than the one we use today but, maybe they contain a flavour which, not only makes them easy to remember, but may even help us to accept the truth which they reveal. In any case it seems quite clear that Julian herself accepted their consoling truth and that, in doing so, she found within herself the strength to keep on living with a certain calm through all the many ups and downs of life. Moreover, as the years went by she came to see and to accept the mystery which her powerful and persistent 'liking'[5] for the God of constant love implied. It was that he himself was somehow actually present in that fundamental 'liking' for him which she had.

God wishes us to know that he keeps us safe all the time, *in woe and in weal.* (LT 15)

I have learned in whatever state I am to be content. (Phil 4:11)

It is not God's will that when we feel pain we should pursue it in sorrow and mourning for it, but that suddenly we should pass it over and preserve ourselves in the endless delight which is God. (LT 15)

Whatever is true, whatever is honourable, whatever is just, whatever is lovely, whatever is gracious, if there is any excellence think about these things. (Phil 4:8)

PASSION AND COMPASSION

After all those unexpected periods of woe within the 'great experience' of Julian, there followed one which brought her to the very point of death. She had been gazing at a crucifix which had been held up by the curate who had come to help her and at this stage it appears to have portrayed for her, not just the sufferings of Christ, but also something of her own. But it did something more. It symbolised the love which made the one whom she saw on the cross do what he did, which was to give his very life for her. Of course, it was in her appreciating that that her desire to do the very same for him developed and grew strong.

As Julian, in her own 'great experience' observed the dying of the one she loved[6] a lot of graphic details flowed across her mind. Some, like his thirst, could have been influenced by memories of Gospel passages. Some others could have come from the embellishments of writers or of preachers of the time.[7] However, one important detail may have been occasioned by the circumstances of East Anglia itself. It was that of the cold and bitter wind which seemed to Julian to dry and shrivel up the dying flesh of Christ.[8] That detail was for Julian a most important one as we will later see but for the moment let us simply note what speaking of it at this stage within her book implied. It was that her own early prayer to see Christ on the cross as Mary and his first disciples did was being answered and, moreover, in a totally involving way.

Let us, however, speak about the 'passion', rather than about the 'sufferings', of Christ because that will allow us to refer with ease to Julian's 'compassion' for the Crucified. 'Compassion' is a good word and, moreover, one which Julian herself quite often used. It means 'to suffer with'[9] and it implies a certain oneness with the one who is in pain. To use it in connection with the way that Julian related to the one whom she saw dying on the cross would, therefore, seem to indicate that she was very much a part of that great devastating moment which she had so earnestly desired to see.

In later life when Julian, already in her anchorhold, became a focus for a lot of people who desired to speak about their problems and their pain, she must have felt some movement of 'compassion' in herself for many of those sufferers as well. Indeed, when writing in a later chapter of the way that people should relate to one another,[10] she implied that that in fact had often been the case. However, when a lot of them had poured out all their worries and their woes she must at times have feared lest her instinctive tendency to be compassionate with them would take her far away from what had been her primary concern, which was to be compassionate with Christ. Yet, on the other hand, she was aware, to some extent at least, that all those movements of compassion which could pull her towards one individual and then towards the next were somehow fundamentally the same as that of her compassion for the Crucified himself. That fact would be much better understood when finally the meaning of her picture-parable, the one about the Servant and the Lord, would be perceived. She, then, would see more clearly than she had before that those who suffer are, in some way, really one with Christ himself and that the One whom she saw on the cross was struggling in each one who came to her. They all, in other words, were part of the one, great, crucifying mystery which in one way or another, was inviting and incorporating her.[11]

As Julian responded to the sufferings of others, she appears to have been greatly helped by thinking about Mary as she stood beside the cross.[12] She stayed there, Julian explained, not in the hope of saving her own son from pain, but just because she could not leave the one she loved so much. Did Julian not often do the same for people whom she knew? Did she not often 'stand by' her afflicted friends although she was aware of just how little she could do. Indeed, at times she must have felt frustrated by her impotence and maybe there were moments when she even felt annoyed. Moreover she must, certainly, have realised what many of us have discovered in the presence of some person in distress: that even words are totally inadequate. Yet, frequently, her very presence and availability to those in need may have been like a welcome sponge which did in fact absorb some of another's crucifying pain.

I saw, in part, the compassion of our Lady, St Mary; for Christ and she were so united in love, that the greatness of her love was the cause of the greatness of her pain. (LT 18)

Standing by the cross of Jesus (was) his mother. (Jn 19:25)

For always, the higher, the stronger, the sweeter that love is, the more sorrow it is to the lover to see the body which he loved in pain. (LT 18)

Look and see if there is any sorrow like my sorrow, which was brought on me. (Lam 1:12)

Now he has risen again and is no longer capable of suffering; and yet he suffers with us. (LT 20)

I rejoice in my sufferings for your sake, and in my flesh I complete what is lacking in the afflictions of Christ, for the sake of his body, that is the church. (Col 1:24)

RELUCTANCE AND DETERMINED CHOICE

Julian, when still quite young, had prayed that she would have the wound of genuine compassion.[13] That she had, at that stage, prayed in such a way could be considered by us as a sign that she already was a sympathetic person, which of course is what we would like to believe. But, be that as it may, her doing so implied that she perceived compassion to be, not just some attractive quality of character which she desired to have but also an important gift which could come only from above. However, since she also spoke about it as a wound, she must have realised that it would be a gift which, paradoxically, could cost her a lot. Her life, as it unfolded, would confirm how true that youthful intuition was.

The great occasion which revealed to Julian how much that spirit of compassion could demand was one which we have had an opportunity to note. It was when everyone around her thought that she was dying and the local curate, who had come, held up a crucifix before her face.[14] Despite her early prayer to be compassionate she did not at that moment want to look at it at all. Although another of her early prayers had been to see the crucified as Mary and his first disciples did,[15] she now seemed to have realised, instinctively, that to decide to look at Jesus as he was upon the cross would be to choose a more demanding route to heaven than the one on which she felt herself to be. However, when that curate had encouraged her a little more, she did agree to make the necessary effort and to look upon the cross and then, with great compassion, on the sufferings which he who died on it endured.

In later life, when Julian was much more conscious of the fact that Christ is somehow 'everyone', the same kind of spontaneous reaction to potential pain may fairly frequently have reoccurred. To offer an example, when some people who were suffering in their own lives came to her anchorhold for consolation or for help, she may at times have been reluctant to receive them or to offer them the welcome they deserved. Perhaps, and here we speculate a little, some may have arrived when she was occupied in some important, even necessary task. Perhaps a number of them came with problems which she knew she could not solve and which she even wanted for some reason to ignore. Perhaps, we speculate again, some others came at moments when she was herself exhausted or not feeling very well. Perhaps. In any case one fact is clear. It is that as she wrote her longer book she made a personal confession. She admitted that there was a moment when she had regretted asking God to grace her with compassion and, indeed, that had she known how much it was to cost her, she might not have asked for it at all.[16] Was she referring then, it could be asked, to that occasion when the curate held a crucifix before her face or to those kinds of situation which I have suggested here? To me it seems that she was probably referring to them all, although the one which was connected with her 'great experience' had certainly become for her symbolic of the rest. Moreover, it seems fairly clear that, just as she had made the effort to accept the Crucified, so she would have done all she could to overcome her later feelings of reluctance and to welcome even those whose struggles worried her or made her somehow conscious of her own.

No doubt, as years went by, she helped a number of such people by her genuine concern, but it would seem that, as she did, she too was helped in no small way by them. Their very coming to her was a challenge which kept her aware of weaknesses which were within herself and waiting to be healed. Indeed their fairly frequent comings may have stimulated her to analyse the split which was within herself and to conclude that her reluctance to become involved came only from some 'outer part' while her desire to be compassionate was symptomatic of an 'inner' and much more important one. That fairly obvious distinction may have left some questions to be answered such as how did her capacity to choose to be compassionate relate to that compassion which could flow from somewhere deep within herself? She would attempt to give some answer to that kind of question later in her life. But, for the moment, to perceive that much in her belonged to just an 'ordinary part', which could, moreover, be controlled and even tamed, must have facilitated her in coping with her fractured personality and in assisting others who came to her anchorhold in pain.

But life could still be hard. The sufferings of those who kept on coming back must have been wearying for Julian, especially as years went by. Indeed, the very social order into which she had been born, and which in many ways must have sustained her, seemed to be collapsing as disputes and organised rebellion started to take place[17] and that too must have worried her. Of course, she would have realised, as she reflected on the dying Christ, that everyone and all creation too would have to share in that disintegrating mystery – but it never is so easy to accept it when it seems to be, not just a theological idea, but an encroaching fact. Yet Julian, in spite of that, was optimistic too. Her deepest grace and inclination was to yearn for life and her determined choice, sustained no doubt beyond the writing of her books and even to the end, seems to have been to welcome it, despite the fact that doing so could mean the total giving of herself.

It came to me that I had little known what pain it was that I had asked, and like a wretch I regretted it, thinking that if I had known what it would be, I should have been reluctant to ask for it. (LT 17)

But Jesus said to James and John: 'you do not know what you are asking. Are you able to drink of the cup that I drink?' (cf. Mk 10:35-38)

Reluctance and deliberate choice are in opposition to one another, and I experienced them both at the same time; and these are two parts, one exterior, the other interior. (LT 19)

I do not understand my own actions, for I do not do what I want but I do the very think I hate. (Rom 7:15)

I truly saw that the interior part is the master and ruler of the exterior, attaching no importance to what the exterior part may will, but forever fixing its intention and will upon being united with our Lord Jesus. (LT 19)

If we live by the Spirit, let us also walk by the Spirit. (Gal 5:25)

It was revealed that the interior part draws the exterior by grace and both will be eternally united in bliss through the power of Christ. (LT 19)

The law of the Spirit of life in Christ Jesus has set me free. (Rom 8:2)

Notes

1. 'This place is prison' wrote Julian in the LT chapter 77. The 'place' most probably referred to her own anchorhold, although she may have also be considering this world in which we have to live until the Day of Resurrection comes.

2. In the Short Text Julian had written: 'This version was shown to me to understand that everybody needs to experience this (i.e. those disconcerting, alternating moods). But in the Long Text what we read is 'some souls profit by experiencing this'. Those who claim that the Long Text is the later one conclude that Julian had here refined an earlier less accurate thought.

3. The fact that she could talk of times when one can be distressed and in the Long Text, say 'although one's sin may not always be the cause' suggests that she was conscious that at other tims we can bring misery upon ourselves. Her emphasis upon contrition in her books, however, would suggest that, when this was the case, her hope would have been for the sufferer to change and so to find the happiness desired.

4. Peter cried out to the Lord: 'Lord, save me, I am perishing'. Only twice did Julian attempt to offer a direct quotation from the scriptures. Both of them are in this present chapter (ST chater 9 & LT chapter 15). One could note that the words of Peter which she provides are in themselves a combination of Mk 8:25 & Mt 14:30.

5. This insight is recorded only in her second book. To understand what is in fact no more than just a brief and unexpected comment let us note that Julian was conscious of the difference, not just between our thinking and our feelings, but between a feeling which she simply liked (ST), or which was even spiritual in itself (LT), and that more fundamental 'lykyng' which she came to see as a participation in that never-ending 'lykyng' which for her was more or less synonymous with God. It was in such a 'lykyng', which she sometimes calls 'delight', that she desired her 'even-christians' to remain.

6. Affective meditation on the Passion was the central devotional activity, not only of professed religious, but of every seriously minded christian

in those medieval days. In this connection, note the words of Margery Kemp who, when an image of Our Lady of Mercy had caused her to weep, said to the local priest: 'his death is as fresh to me as if he had died this very day and so I think it ought to be to you and to all christian people'. (cf. *The Book of Margery Kempe*. S. B. Meech & H. E. Allen (Eds), EETS, 1940).

7. *The Meditations on the Passion* by Julian's near contemporary Richard Rolle, as well as other books were read to Margery Kempe by her own spiritual directors. Perhaps some similar books were read or loaned to Julian too.

8. The reference to the 'charcoal fire because it was cold' which we find in Jn 18:18 may have commenced a train of thought. However, it is difficult to think that an acute awareness of that cold, east wind which blew through Norwich every winter did not influence the words of many preachers and, indeed the words of Julian herself.

9. 'Passion comes from the Latin *patior* (I suffer) and compassion from *cum-patior* (I suffer with). One could add that 'sympathy' means much the same, though coming ultimately, not from Latin, but from Greek.

10. cf. 'For the contemplation of the sins of others makes a thick mist before the soul's eye and during that time we cannot see the beauty of God unless we contemplate them with contrition, compassion and with holy desires to God for him' (cf. LT chapter 76).

11. cf. ST chapter 1 & LT chapter 2. Her second prayer was to receive a bodily sickness so severe that she would think that she was just about to die. That was, in fact, what happened to her at the age of 30½. However, as she came to understand her own vocation in the context of the whole community (that is the church) this dying would have been repeated as she contemplated and responded to the sufferings of even-christians whom she knew.

12. There was much devotion to our Lady in those medieval days and quite a lot of it was focussed on her sorrows. But her sorrows were connected with the sufferings of Christ and so devotion to our Lady would have led the devotee to him. However, once again, one must consider the effects of Julian's belated understanding of her picture-parable. Just as it helped her to see Christ in everyone who suffered, so it made it possible for her to see in Mary one who could encourage her as she tried to respond to all her even-christians when they were in pain.

13. The third and most important of the early prayers of Julian was for a triple gift. Its first part was for true contrition while the second, and the one which now concerns us in this section, was compassion and the third, the gift for a longing with the will for God. (cf. ST chapter 1 & LT chapter 2)

14. cf. ST chapter 2 & LT chapter 3.

15. cf. ST chapter 1 & LT chapter 2.

16. cf. LT chapter 17 (cf. LT chapter 19).

17. Against the background of the Peasants' Revolt and the subsequent disturbance in society, it is interesting to read what Julian wrote about the failing of all things. *All creatures which God created for our service failed in their natural functions* (LT chapter 18). This is a passage which has been expanded in the Longer Text and it is tempting to suppose that it was all the failing social circumstances of her time which had occasioned her reflection here. However, while that must remain conjecture, it may be of interest to observe that Julian, while contemplating Christ, was also able to refer to God's powerful, *secret preservation of (those creatures)* too.

We now come to the second part of this climactic mystery, that which shows the new life we are all invited to to enjoy.

The 'Showings' which concern us here are four: the 9th, the 10th, the 11th and the 12th.

The commentaries of Julian which offer us our chosen themes are those contained in ST chapter 12 and half of the one which follows and in the LT chapters 21-26.

JOY & DELIGHT

Suddenly he was completely changed! He, who had been close to death, now seemed so very much alive.To say that Julian was taken by surprise would be an understatement. She had been prepared to see him die and so the transformation which she saw astonished her. But at the same time, as she saw it, she was also filled with unexpected happiness and joy.

In reading through this section of the books of Julian I always feel that something else could have been said. In other words, while she asserted that it was the change in Christ which caused the change which happened in herself, could her recovery not have been caused by other factors too? Could we not, for example, say that it was the result of some improvement in her physical condition or, perhaps, of her own fundamental urge to live. This second proposition, since it is connected with the kind of person that she was, may be worthwhile exploring and, in order to corroborate it, let me offer here two bits of circumstantial evidence. The first is that when Julian had prayed for an experience of dying, as she did, it was not for a dying unto death but for a dying which would bring her only to its opening doors and then, allow her to recover and to live.[1] The second is that Julian who must have worked both hard and constantly to write her books was clearly a determined person and at thirty-and-a-half the strength of her determination may have been enough to tip the scales when otherwise she might have died. In consequence, can we not argue that the cause of her recovery was also in herself. In that case the amazing change which seemed to happen in the Christ-like figure whom she saw would have not been the cause of her recovery but its result. However, it could also be

considered as a sign of her conviction that the life which she received came ultimately from the Source of life itself.

How Julian became aware of this new life which she was
then receiving was through all that joy which she had in herself.
Indeed, as she recorded in her shorter book, she felt at that time
that she was as 'glad and merry' as it would be possible to be.[2]
The primary reason for that wonderful sensation was, according
to herself, that she was being loved by God and in a way which
she had never known before. That was, as we have seen, the ker-
nel and very essence of her 'great experience' and she would
treasure it through all the years ahead. But for the moment all
her concentration seems to have been on the 'joy' which that
great love had caused and which appears to have exploded at
that moment into an extreme 'delight'. Indeed, while joy can
often be a quiet if sustaining quality of life, it seems that, as she
gazed upon the figure of the suddenly transfigured Christ, it
was igniting every fibre of her being.

As Julian was, as it were, caught up in this delight she seems
to have been conscious that it was enabling her to understand
the wondrous life which is that of the Trinity itself. She certainly,
while trying to describe her joy, associated it both with the
Father and the Son and then, although much less explicitly, with
their own Spirit of delight. No doubt, we will be able to detect in
what she wrote the influence of christian teaching which she
had received but, if we do, let us acknowledge also one important fact: that her incorporation of the doctrine of the Trinity into
her understanding of her own experience enabled her to understand the Trinity itself with more excitement than is frequently
the case. The Father, for example, was for her a person totally
delighted with the Son because he had so well expressed the
love he had received, and for the benefit of all. The Son, in turn,
was seen by her as equally delighted since he had received as his
reward the gift he wanted most, which was of course, not only
Julian herself, but also all those whom his everlasting Father
loved. As for the Holy Spirit, it appears to have been that 'delight' personified[3] and so, for Julian, the Person of the Trinity
who seemed to be encompassing, personifying and explaining,

hers. In realising that, however, she was, as her very words suggest, exceptionally graced.

Since Julian's description of this mystery in which she was so involved may seem to some to be at this point in her book a little rarefied, it may be useful to conclude this section on a much more manageable note. I have in mind one sentence which she wrote and which must have consoled and cheered her in the years which lay ahead. It says that, in relation to the Christ whom she perceived as so delighted, we are no less than 'his bliss and his reward, his honour and his crown'. Of course, as we have noted, Julian could make that kind of statement with conviction since in her own vision she had seen, not only that we are being given by the Father to the Son, but also that we are the very gift which he so much desires. However, for most people it would probably be easier to understand that he, who is so full of life, could be our bliss and our reward, than that we could be his.[4] Indeed, the only way to come to terms with its amazing opposite would be to recognise and to accept the fact that it is his transforming Spirit which is active in our lives.

I watched with all my might for the moment when Christ would expire but I did not see him so ... suddenly, as I looked at the same cross, he changed to an appearance of joy. The change in his appearance changed mine, and I was as glad and joyful as I could possibly be. (LT 21)

And as he was praying the appearance of his countenance was altered and his raiment became dazzling white. ...Peter said to Jesus: 'Master, it is well that we are here'. (Lk 9:19-33)

We are his bliss, we are his reward, we are his honour, we are his crown. And this was a singular wonder and a most delectable contemplation, that we are his crown. (LT 22)

The church, which is his body, the fullness of him who fills all in all. (Eph 1:23)

INTO THE HEART

The heart is a symbol of love. The heart of Jesus, consequently, has become, for those who have the eyes of faith, the symbol of a love which is divine. However, for a lot of people in the world today this latter symbol has no longer its once captivating power. Perhaps it has become too gaudy in the way that it has frequently been shown. Perhaps it has become associated with a sentimental kind of love which does not really satisfy. In any case 'the heart of Jesus' did not have such problems for the people of the fourteenth century or for Julian herself. They lived before the age of cheap, repository art and, while they would have heard their preachers speak about the 'heart of Jesus', they would have accepted it for what it was: a metaphor which seemed to promise them the love which they did not deserve but very much desired.

Before we let ourselves explore this thought, it might be of some use to note one element in what became a popular devotion to the Sacred Heart, if only to eliminate it here. It is that element of reparation which has been associated in a special way with Margaret Mary Alocoque,[5] that Visitation nun who lived three hundred years ago in France. For her the 'heart of Jesus' symbolised, not just a love which is divine but also one which was rejected by so many of the people of her time. In consequence, what seemed to her important was, not only to rejoice in being loved, but also to do all she could to make up for the sins of those who did not let that love affect and sanctify their lives. While not denying all the good which this new emphasis provoked, it must be said that it could also make the love of Christ seem less important to devotees of the Sacred Heart than what they did themselves. It could, moreover, even make them think of Jesus as dependent on their efforts without recognising that those very efforts had no value without his. Indeed without him they could not do anything at all.[6] But Julian who lived before this 'reparation movement' (and before the age of the pathetic Jesus of repository art!) was able to accept with simple gratitude the love which Christ seemed always ready to provide.

Since Julian believed that she was loved so totally by Christ, it is not too surprising to discover that she thought about that very special gospel verse which speaks of blood and water flowing from his side.[7] This had been, in the early and the medieval church, a verse which was much used to indicate the love in which the church itself was born and it was often used to illustrate the grace of baptism and of the eucharist as well. But here, what Julian desired to say was simply that she was herself receiving and enjoying at that very moment in her 'great experience' that life which seemed to flow abundantly from him. It should be noted here, however, that, as she perceived the greatness and the wonder of that life which is beyond what any human words can say,[8] her yearning for it grew. She, therefore, seems to have consoled herself, especially perhaps in dry and barren moments, with the stimulating thought that God would not refuse a prayer for more of that life-giving love which he himself so lovingly desired her to receive.

As Julian reflected on this opened 'heart of Jesus' she was fascinated by the fact that it seemed to contain within itself a fair and lovely place. It was a place, moreover, which attracted her and which she felt a great desire to enter and, indeed, to live in as her everlasting home. In this she could have been encouraged by the way that preachers may have spoken, since the wish to go into the heart of Jesus was a cultivated aspiration of the time.[9] However, what may be of interest to us here is that to speak of entering his heart is fundamentally the same as to refer to entering a castle[10] or some other place which is of circular design. They all suggest a haven which is safe and promising of peace. Of course, since Julian referred a little earlier to God enfolding her (a way of speaking which suggests that, at that moment, she may have been cosily surrounded by her clothes), she must have had already some of the advantages of that all-perfect haven which for her was still to come. However, what she wanted to communicate as she reflected on the open and inviting heart was that she had no doubt at all but that her hope of reaching and of being in such a delightful place would one day be fulfilled. Moreover, she was certain that, because she saw it in the heart of Christ, she would enjoy when she arrived, not only rest and peace, but also all the benefits of being totally enfolded in the love of One who is himself divine.

As Julian continued to reflect on that most pleasant place which she saw in the 'heart of Jesus' she recalled that it seemed large enough for all who would be saved. That kind of statement, when she said it, was, one must admit, a cautious one since it did not imply that everybody would be saved but, at the same time, it avoided saying that there would be anyone who would be left outside. But Julian was one who loved to dance upon the brink of what could be described as 'total inclusivity' and probably she hoped that all those people who would read her books would learn to do the same. However, her reflections on the all-embracing love which was suggested by the open 'heart of Jesus' must have had some very practical results as well. They must have helped her to see everyone who came to her as one who could, with her, become a dweller of that favoured place. Moreover, they must have encouraged her to do all that she could for them so that they would more easily attain that 'fair, delectable place', that paradise of everlasting peace, for which they also had been made.

(Our good Lord) brought to mind the dear and precious blood and water which he suffered to be shed for love. (LT 24)	One of his soldiers pierced his side and at once there came out blood and water. (Jn 19:34)
Our good Lord gazed with joy and with his sweet regard he drew his creature's understanding into his side by the same wound. (LT 24)	Jesus stood up and proclaimed: If anyone is thirsty, let him come to me and let him who believes in me come to me and drink. As Scripture says: 'Out of his heart shall flow rivers of living water'. (Jn 7:35)

... and there he revealed a fair and delectable place, large enough for all that will be saved and will rest in peace and in love. (LT 24)

Come to me and I will give you rest; for I am gentle and lowly of heart and you will find rest for your souls. (Mt 11:28-29)

For my greater understanding these blessed words were said: See how I love you... How could it be that you would pray for me for anything pleasing to me which I would not very gladly grant to you? (LT 24)

Ask and you will receive. (Mt.7:7)

My people will abide in a peaceful habitation, in secure dwellings and in quiet resting places. (Is 32:18)

MARY

It could be said that Mary did not play a major part in Julian's spirituality. She is referred to in her books but there are only three occasions where she features in a truly captivating way, and even then the passages concerned are relatively short. Yet each of those three passages, and all of them together, indicate that, if her part was not the central one, it was important and, moreover, such that it can tell us quite a lot about the personality of Julian herself.

The first time Julian referred to Mary was quite early in her book. It was when she depicted her as marvelling because her own Creator had desired, not only to be born of humankind, but to be born of her.[11] In that, of course, she had been influenced by the 'Annunciation' story which had been a favourite with Christians ever since the time it was composed.[12] Perhaps that was because they all saw something in it of themselves! In any case, when Julian herself reflected on that story, she became aware of some affinity between herself and Mary. Both were people who could marvel at that wonderful yet very humbling truth: That God who is so very great should come to them who were so very small.

The second time that Julian referred to Mary was when she was pondering the crucifixion scene.[13] We have already noted that occasion. We have seen how Julian considered her, who stood beside the crucified, to be a model for herself as she, within the context of her own vocation, tried to do the same. Indeed, that model of compassion must have frequently been reproduced throughout the years as people brought their sufferings to Julian and found in her a loyal and supportive friend.

The third occasion was when Julian herself was filled with resurrection joy. In that condition she perceived the woman who had stood beside the cross as 'high and noble' and indeed as 'glorious'. The maiden, who had welcomed Christ into her womb, was now seen in a spiritual way as sharing in that life of happiness which was already his. Indeed, since Julian could speak of Mary as 'Our Lady', as was normal in those feudal times, it could be said that she perceived her at that moment as the spiritual spouse of him whom feudal christians had begun to speak of as 'our Lord'. But let us for a little while put that particular thought aside. Instead, let us consider here that more involving truth: that Julian, in seeing Mary so transformed, was not just contemplating all the joy that Mary was presumed to have but also an expression for her own.

These three distinct, but somewhat similar, appeals to Mary raise a certain question which may be of interest to us here. It is: 'did Julian have what could be thought of as a real devotion to "Our Lady" or should we consider her relationship with Mary in some other way?' Indeed, because there are so many different attitudes to Mary in the Christian world today, to ascertain the quality of Julian's relationship with her may help a lot of Christians to assess the value of their own. Moreover, it may help those Christians who would claim to have a Marian devotion to appreciate their own relationship with Mary in a context which will illustrate the nature of her greatness and, in consequence, of theirs.

We therefore ask: 'did Julian have a Marian devotion?' One has to admit that Julian herself has not left many indications that she did. However, one remark within her shorter book implies that she addressed some prayers to Mary every day,[14] as would have been the custom with most Christians of her time. Moreover, in her longer book she made an effort to explain that she did not have any problem in allowing those whom God had given her as mediators to assist her in whatever way they could[15] and, of those people, Mary would, of course, have been by far the most important one. But does that prove that Julian herself had what could be considered as a Marian devotion? All that I can say for certain is that, since she sympathetically tells us in the chapter which concerns us here that Christ himself desired his mother to be loved, we have sufficient reason to presume that Julian, in her own loving way, loved Mary as a person too.

While Julian may well have had a warm devotion to 'Our Lady', it would seem that Mary, to a large extent, was understood by her, not only as an individual to be admired and loved, but also as a symbol of herself. She was so, as we have already noted, when she was perceived as marvelling that he who was so great should come to her who was so small. She was so when she was perceived as standing by the cross of one who suffered much and now on this, the third, occasion she appears to have reflected something of the dignity which Julian discovered in herself. Did she not tell us that the Lord himself seemed to enquire of her: 'Do you desire to see in Mary how much you are loved?' Thus Mary must have been, or more and more must have become, for Julian, not just a person who was to be loved, but a consoling symbol of herself as being loved, as well. In consequence it could be said that in her case *devotion to* became subsumed into a greater and more intimate relationship, one of *identifying with*.

But Mary, as a symbol, seems to have meant something more. As Julian reflected on the glory which she saw in her, she came to realise that she personified, not just herself, but all the faithful as a great community, especially as it will be when filled with that same glory in the world which is to come. Thus Mary was for her the living symbol of the church in much the same way as some other female figures have become the symbols of some other kinds of group. The Irish, for example, have had their own Róisín Dubh and then, more recently, their wonderful Caitlín Ní hUalihan while British people have proclaimed the glories of Britannia. Of course there was a difference too, for Mary was an individual in her own right as well as the symbolic figure for a very special group. But what could be of interest and of value to us is to know that, in perceiving Mary as a symbol of the church, our anchoress was following in her own loving way, a strong tradition which goes back to very early Christian times and which has found again an echo in our own.[16]

There is one other thought which could be mentioned here. It is that Mary, either as an individual or as a symbol of the human race, should always be considered in conjunction with the One from whom her glory comes. Perhaps, however, we are now beginning to pursue a thought which goes beyond the area of Julian's immediate concern. Yet, in a later chapter of her longer book, there is one section which suggests that what I have in mind may not have been completely foreign to her thought. That section, which concludes her explanation of her picture-parable about a servant and his lord, implies that this important thought about not isolating Mary does in fact deserve to be included here.

That passage to which I refer appears to speak of Christ himself as sitting at the right hand of the Father in the glory which will be forever his. But that same passage also tells us that beside him there was seen by Julian 'a maiden fair of endless joy' who was 'his own beloved wife'.[17] That 'maiden fair' and 'wife' was certainly for her an image of the church itself when, in the fullness of the resurrection, it will be completely one with Christ and fully sharing in the glory which he has himself received. But, when we think about that mystery with the mind of Julian herself, does not her vision of that 'maiden fair' seem to include the vision which she had of Mary as the spiritual spouse of Christ? If that is so, can we not say that Mary, whom she honoured as 'Our Lady', is the one who, next to him who is 'our

Lord', expresses in her own reflected glory what we all one day will be and also what, in some degree at least, we all already are.

I understood the reverent contemplation with which she beheld her God, who is her Creator, marvelling with great reverence that he was willing to be born of her . (LT 4)

And the angel said: Do not be afraid, Mary, for you have found favour with God... The Holy Spirit will come-upon you and the power of the Most High will over-shadow you.(Lk 1:30-35)

I saw in part the compassion of our Lady, St Mary. (LT 18)

Standing by the cross of Jesus was his mother. (Jn 19:25)

Just as before I had seen her small and simple, now he showed her high and noble and glorious. (LT 25)

A great sign appeared in heaven, a woman clothed with the sun,with the moon under her feet and, on her head, a crown of twelve stars. (Rev 12:1)

And our good Lord said: 'Do you wish to see in her how you are loved?' (LT.25)

I looked, and behold a great multitude, from every tribe and nation, standing before the Lamb (cf. Rev 7:9)

BEYOND

The 'Showing' which appears to be a climax to the ones which we have pondered was of Christ, but in a glory which was totally beyond what any human eye could see. It was indeed, it seems to me, quite similar to that final apparition in the gospel story which, according to St Matthew, took place on a mountainside in Galilee.[18] On that occasion the magnetic presence of the risen Christ was recognised in such a powerful way that those who had assembled there could do no more than silently adore. In

any case, the Christ, whom Julian had visualised a little while
before, now seemed to her to merge into that indescribable and
everlasting being which her inmost self desired. He had, indeed,
become for her: the Lord. He had become the Kyrios, the
Yahweh of the biblical tradition or, in other words, the one who
could proclaim: 'I am who am.'

But let us look more closely at the words which he is said by
Julian to have proclaimed. They were not, just 'I am', but something which is surely more intriguing. They were '*I it am*'. Thus,
she did not hear Christ say to her at that moment 'I am he' (as
modern translations can imply). Nor did she hear him tell her 'I
am she' (although she would have much to say about Christ as a
Mother later on). Instead, she seemed to hear him utter what she
took to be a totally transcendent '*it*', an '*it*' which is not either
male nor female even though it could be thought of as including
both. Christ, therefore, had become for her absorbed into the
very mystery of the all-transcending deity itself.

When Julian reflected on that awesome moment she recalled
that it was also one in which she had been filled with unexpected
and surpassing joy. Indeed, so great was her delight that she felt,
as it were, compelled to share with all her 'even-Christians' all
the insights which she had received so that they too might, then,
experience the same.[19] However, it would seem that, as she tried
to find the magic words, she gradually recognised a sobering
but very salutary truth. It was that, even though she so much
wanted to assist those people to discover all the happiness
which they could also have, there was in fact so little she could
do. She, therefore, had no option but to trust that God himself,
who had already done so much for her, would touch their hearts
as well and, thereby, lead them through her feeble words (and
through their merely human thoughts)[20] into that joyful and
love-giving mystery of his own transcendent life.

Indeed, it must have been because she realised that that, in
fact, was what was happening to so many of her visitors and
friends that Julian began to recognise, more clearly than she ever
had before, another and a most important truth. This time it was

that all her 'even-Christians', and not only those who had become professional 'contemplatives', were being called by God into the fullness of a wonderful and liberating life.[21] Indeed, as she would later see, it was, not only all those 'even-Christians', but all people everywhere who are invited to receive that life which only a transcendent deity possesses and can give.[22]

Again and again our Lord said: 'I it am. I it am who is the highest. I it am whom you love. (LT 26)	The eleven disciples went to Galilee, to the mountain to which Jesus directed them. And, when they saw him they worshipped him. (Mt 28:16-17)

Notes

1. cf. ST. chapter 2 & LT. chapter 3
2. cf. ST. chapter 12
3. 'Delight', or rather 'lykyng', was a special word for Julian. While 'joy' is something one can have, 'delighting' or, to use her own word, 'lykyng' indicates the presence of another, One delights in something or in somebody outside oneself and 'lykyng' indicates the same. Thus these words are relational. For Julian, moreover, they implied the Holy Spirit since for her that Spirit was the bond which *ones* us both to Christ and to the Father. It may be of interest to observe again that earlier when Julian was saying that we should preserve ourselves in 'endless lykyng' she then added that that 'lykyng' indicated God. (cf. LT chapter 15). In chapter 23, more consciousof the Trinity, she said, with greater accuracy, that that 'lykyng' was the Holy Spirit.
4. Anthony de Mello SJ has an exercise for prayer in his most useful book *Sadhana* which could be considered here. He tells his readers to re-call the titles of affection which, within a previous exercise, they had ap-

plied to God (such as 'my rock', 'my shield', 'my joy', 'my love') and to imagine God now saying them to us. He then admits that many people find this exercise quite difficult to do.

5. Margaret Mary Alacoque (1647-1690) was a Visitation nun of Paray-le-Moniale in France who claimed to have received some revelations which concerned devotion to the Sacred Heart. Although her primary message was about the love of God, there was another aspect which in fact became increasingly important in her life. It was that of the need to make some reparation for the sins which are committed every day and, consequently, she herself began to undertake extraordinary penances.

6. cf. Jn 15:4-5

7. cf. Jn 19:34.

8. Note Julian's statement at the end of her Long Text, chapter nine: 'I may not and cannot show the spiritual visions as plainly and fully as I would wish. But I trust in our Lord God almighty that he will, out of his goodness and love for you, make you accept it more spiritually and more sweetly than I can or may tell it'.

9. The following sentences are taken from the Franciscan Saint Bonaventure, who was still an influential author at that time. 'Since we have come to the most sweet heart of Jesus and since it is good to dwell therein, let us not carelessly depart... How good it is and agreeable to dwell within this heart... O Jesus, they have pierced your side but it has opened up for us a way into your heart'.

10. St Teresa of Avila, for example, used the image of a castle to explain the spiritual life. She even called her most developed study *The Interior Castle*.

11. cf. ST chapter 4 & LT chapter 4.

12. cf. Lk 1:26-38.

13. ST chapter 10 & LT chapter 18.

14. cf. ST chapter 19.

15. LT chapter 6.

16. In the early church, Mary was considered as the image or the 'type' of the whole community. In the Middle Ages, as devotion to her as an individual developed, her symbolic role was often less appreciated and quite easily overlooked. In recent times, however, she has once again been honoured as a 'type' or symbol of the church, especially through documents produced and promulgated at the second Vatican Council.

17. cf. LT chapter 51 (last paragraph)

18. Mt 28:16-17.

19. 'I was greatly moved in love towards my fellow-christians, that

they may all see and know the same as I saw, for I wished it to be a comfort for them, for all this vision was shown for all' (cf. LT chapter 8)

20. Note Julian's own admission in this chapter that what she perceived surpassed her own 'intelligence and understanding and her powers.'

21. In the Short Text Julian had written that every contemplative soul who seeks will find God in their contemplation. That restriction is omitted in the Longer Text in keeping with her intuition that the love of God is offered, not to them alone, but to us all.

22. The picture-parable of the Servant and the Lord implies that everyone is represented by that Servant who is Christ. At that point Julian accepts a universal fellowship in which the Father sees his Son in everyone and in the Spirit welcomes all.

Part Three

The Mystery of Sin

A cloth hung up to dry

The 13th 'Showing' is quite different from the others. It concerns the barrier or gap which is between ourselves and God and which, within her 'great experience' was seen by Julian to be within herself as well. In other words it showed her something of the mystery which is known as 'sin' but, at the same time, it revealed the welcome and consoling truth that it will someday, somehow, be completely overcome.

Her commentary on this begins half way through chapter 13 of her Shorter Text and then continues to the end of the 18th. Within the longer one it runs inclusively from chapter 27 on to 40.

Sin

Sin!

What is it? We have noted that, according to one point of view, it is 'no thing' at all.[1] It was, of course, when Julian had realised that God is present everywhere that she became aware that his ubiquity implied that there was nowhere left for sin. That was a very metaphysical perception but it was, as well, a most consoling one and so it is not too surprising to discover that it surfaces at this stage in her writings once again. However, let us keep it to the side and focus for the moment on the other and more common point of view.

This other way of understanding sin is to consider it as 'doing what should not be done or as not doing what one should'. That certainly appears to be a much more practical approach and yet, despite its doubtless value, it is one which could reveal some limitations too. For instance, it could indicate that 'sin' is no more than a crime (a legal term) or even that it is no more than just a mere mistake. However, without slipping back into her metaphysical perspective, let us find, with Julian, some kind of working definition which will situate it for us it in a moral (not a legal) setting and, in consequence, with reference to God.

Since Julian believed that God is good, she could declare that sin, to the extent that it exists, must be the very opposite and therefore, to adopt her own expression, 'all that is not good'. That quasi-definition may in fact have been for many of her visitors a useful step to understanding sin because most people at that time would have agreed that there was much that was not good within society and some, no doubt, would have admitted that there was a lot that was not good within themselves as well. Indeed, some chapters later, Julian will name for us some elements in her own character which she perceived as 'not good' in themselves and so as hindrances in her relationship with God.[2] We will discuss those elements in another place but, for the moment, let us simply note that it was her desire for union with that God of goodness which made her, not only quick to recognise all that was not good in herself, but also ready to do all she could to let such undesirable components disappear.

For some of those who came to Julian for help, however, their own situation must have seemed to them much more precarious than hers. Indeed, if their own personal experience of life had been predominantly one of suffering (and suffering in those days was often very great) they would have found it easy to presume that suffering was sent by God as punishment for sin, and maybe in particular for theirs. From such a dark belief it would have been quite easy for them to conclude that God himself must be an angry god and, maybe, one who frequently could be vindictive too.[3] However, people of that kind would soon have sensed, perhaps with some relief, that Julian was ill at ease with such assumptions and that she had others of her own. Yet all that she could do to help them may have been to fall back on her own experience and to express her own unshakable conviction that God cannot be annoyed or angry since he is in fact all-love. That may, of course, have led her to suggest to some that, if they could begin to think of their own sufferings in another and more manageable way, they might begin to find within themselves what they so much desired: some indications of God's presence and concern which could encourage them in their own fundamental search, which was for no less than an ever-greater unity with him.

As I read through this section of the books of Julian, I sometimes wonder if the questions which are indicated in the text came only from herself or also from those visitors who desperately felt the need to find some meaning for their troubled lives. 'If God is all-love, as you say,' some may have asked, 'why does he let such painful happenings occur?' while others may in some way have demanded: 'why does God who sees all things before they happen not prevent all tragedies when opportunities arise?' To questions such as those she had, of course, no fully satisfying answers. Therefore, it might not be too surprising to discover that on some occasions she could say, perhaps in desparation, that, since God who is all-love does not blame us, there is at least no point in those who suffer blaming him.[4] However, she could well have added at such moments that, if she could not explain why certain things had happened in the past, she had no doubt at all that, since God is not only powerful but all-loving, – 'all things in the future will be well.[5]

But sin itself retained for Julian its unresolved and tantalising mystery.

It was 'nothing', like an empty gap or like a hole dug in the ground.[6] But, at the same time, she was able to imagine it as some kind of a 'hindrance' which implies that it is 'something' which can be removed. Moreover, as she intimated on a few occasions, she was also able to describe it as a stain. This last idea, in fact, may have had quite a strong appeal since Julian would have remembered that, within her 'great experience' Christ seemed to wash her with his over-flowing blood.[7] Indeed it may have been that very thought of being cleansed which led her to another and, indeed, exciting one. It was that she herself, beneath the stains of all or any sin, was no less than the very image of the living and the loving God.[8] Yet, even as she marvelled at that very thought, she was concerned about that staining and impeding mystery which remained and so she kept on longing for the day when it would be no more and she completely free.

Our Lord brought to my mind the longing that I had for him before and I saw that nothing hindered me but sin. (LT 27)	I am sure that neither death nor life… nor anything else in all creation will be able to separate us from the love of God in Christ Jesus our Lord. (Rom 8:38-39)

I often wondered why, through the great prescient wisdom of God, the beginning of sin was not prevented. (LT 27)	But who are you to answer back to God? What, will the moulded say to the moulder 'why have you made me thus?' (Rom 9:20)
Sin is necessary but all will be well, and all will be well and every kind of thing will be well. (LT 27)	We know that in everything God works for good with those who love him. (Rom 8:28)

THE DYING CHURCH

The news was not inspiring. Had the media of today been active then, the headlines could have been quite shattering. One paper, for example, might have screamed that: 'Popes fight for the papal throne!', referring to the schism which had taken place and to the rivalry between opposing sides.[9] Another paper might have printed: 'Bishop and his followers defeated' when the Norwich Bishop, who had fought for his own candidate came back from battle in disgrace. Then, on some other day, a piece of local news: 'A heretic burnt at the Lollards' Pit'. The church in many ways was in a bad condition and while, certainly, there were some signs of genuine Christian life, they hardly were the topics chosen by the people for their ordinary gossip every day. Julian, however, did not write about such things and so we have to go to other sources when we want to find the social background to her life. Yet, as we read her longer book, it does become quite obvious that she was very much aware that all was not well with the church. Indeed, in one place she appears to say that, if it was already sick and suffering, it would get even worse.[10] Perhaps it was because her life was operating at a deep and spiritual level that she was so very sensitive, not only to the imperfections of her church, but even to its constant and inherent weakness too. Perhaps. In any case, it surely must have been that life which made it possible for her to see the

goodness which it also had and to be sure that that same goodness had within itself the power which it required to grow.

Perhaps, a lot of those who made their way to Julian were
genuinely worried and concerned about the imperfections
which they saw within their church. If so, some could have
asked her: 'how can they be remedied?' or 'is it even possible to
give life to a dying church?' or, entering the practical domain,
'what, therefore, should we do?' Those questions were not only
valid ones but urgent at the time and, after all the reformations
which have been attempted since that period, they are the questions which we have to keep on asking still. However, Julian
herself does not appear to have suggested any formula which,
being followed, would remove the scandals of her time and,
consequently, heal their sick and dying church.[11] But, on the
other hand, she must have made a real and most important contribution to its betterment both by the guidance which she gave
to those who wanted it and by the silent witness of her dedicated
life. Indeed, it could be argued that, if her own contribution had
been more appreciated by all those who knew of her existence,
and her warlike bishop would have been included in that group,
then Christian life would have been better in the diocese of
Norwich than it was. One could, moreover, push that argument
a little further and declare that, if her teaching had been more accepted, then the still remaining problems in the church would
have been much more easily addressed and some might even
have been solved.

It seems to me that Julian's own attitude, and so her contribution, to the church had been assisted by one insight in particular
which she already had. It was that 'sin', however it may be described, was only in what seemed to her to be the 'outer part' of
human nature and that, consequently, there remained an 'inner
part' which it did not affect at all.[12] Those two parts, at the time
of her own 'great experience', she had perceived as being in herself, and seeing that must have become for her a cause for much
encouragement and hope. However, at a later stage, she seems
to have presumed, not only that those parts were in her 'even-

Christians' too, but also that they were the indispensable components of the Christian church itself. In other words, she came to realise that in the church there was that same mysterious 'inner part' which is in every individual and which, as Julian had also seen, is always able to control the outer one and then to draw it to itself. Thus Julian, we can conclude, had reason to accept her less than perfect church and, at the same time, to believe that its myserious, 'inner part' could change it into that ideal community which she and everyone desired.

In this connection, let us note an image which apparently came to the mind of Julian as she was gazing on the figure on the cross. It was that of a piece of cloth which had been hung up in the air to dry. At first, it seemed to her, to represent the crucified as he was going though the anguishes of death.[13] But later, as her understanding grew, she realised that it was symbolising Christ, not only as he was on Calvary, but also as he suffered in his torn and battered church.[14] However, in her visionary faith she could see something else. It would take many years of pondering before she put it into words but, when she did, it was to indicate that what she saw appeared to be, no piece of dry and shrivelled cloth, but one which was a rich and royal robe.[15] A splendid and enticing sign! Indeed, it could be said that it must often have been through such powerful images that Julian helped many people of her time. Moreover some, like this one, may help people of our own, not only to accept the sinful church of which they are imperfect members, but to realise what, with the grace of God, it certainly can be.

Our Lord ... imposes on every person whom he loves ... something that is no defect in his sight, through which some souls are humiliated and despised in this world. (LT 28)	It is better to suffer for doing what is right, if that should be God's will, than for doing wrong. For Christ also died for sins. (1 Pet 3:17-18)

Holy Church will be shaken in sorrow and anguish and tribulation in this world, as men shake a cloth in the wind. (LT 28)	When you hear of wars and rumours of wars do not be alarmed; this must take place but the end is not yet. (Mk 13:7)
Then our mortal flesh, which was Adam's old tunic, was made lovely, new and bright, forever clean... so marvellous that I can never describe it. (LT 51)	The fine linen is the righteous deeds of the saints. (Rev 19:8)

A GREAT DEED TO BE DONE

The problem still remained. On one side, so it seemed to Julian, there was the weight of her own personal experience which said that God was all the time enfolding her, and wanting to enfold all others too. But, on the other side, there were the many pains and suffering which we encounter in our lives and, then, inevitable death. All that seemed to suggest that, far from always loving and enfolding us, God could be absent, even angry or vindictively enraged. How then could all be well? The question kept on taunting Julian and, even though she obviously had a good and very probing mind,[16] she could not see how God could cope with all those obstacles and so make all things well.

Her problem was of course compounded by the adverse weight of the apparent teaching of the church. It spoke of people who were damned, or could be so, for all eternity. In fact, it would appear that what she actually heard was that the Jews, the pagans and all christians who did not live as they should were destined to be part of that unenviable group. That must have been a saddening and a terrifying thought for anyone and, certainly, it must have seemed to Julian to contradict her deep conviction and desire that all things would be well. But what was she to do? Perhaps, she may have thought, if she were to discover what the church's teaching really was, it might appear more nuanced and more manageable that what many of its preachers actually said.

It may have been because she did investigate the more authentic teaching of the church that she was able to present her own ideas as confidently as she did. Thus, when she spoke about the Jews, she was prepared to make provision for all those who were converted by the saving grace of God. Of course, she did not say how many those would be but she had obviously shied away from judging them by what some others may have said. Her preference was to judge them, not as people who seemed to reject the grace of God, but in the light of his all-powerful love. In that way she could keep in her own mind a door for them ajar.

It is, perhaps, a pity that she did not speak about the pagans in that same kind of redeeming way but, then, it is unlikely that she would have known too many or that they would have impinged themselves too urgently upon her mind. However, when it came to mentioning the baptised Christians who would not be saved she did show some unease with having only one disqualifying clause. She, therefore, spoke of them, not only as not having lived good, Christian lives, but also as, to quote her, 'dying out of charity' as well. Again of course she never said how many would or would not be in that despondent category but let us note the phrase she chose to use. It was one which would have allowed her to enjoy the thought that God, whose charity is infinite, would never let one of his loved ones to be lost. Another door was, thereby, left ajar.[17]

That only left the devils which, according to church's teaching, seemed forever damned. It would appear from what she wrote that Julian accepted that. But since she was so confident that God is, not just good, but everywhere, one cannot help but wonder if she sometimes wondered if God's powerful love would not in some way touch and save them too!

As Julian reflected on these problems and, no doubt, discussed them with some learned visitors, solutions of a kind came to her mind.

The first one seems to echo scripture when it spoke of those whose names would be no longer in the book of life.[18] What Julian herself declared was that they would not be as much as even mentioned in the presence of the God-of-all or of his gathered saints! But what exactly could that mean? It seems to me, to say the least, that it could be considered in the light of something which most people on occasions do. That is to blot out from their minds those elements in life which worry them in order to get on with other and more energising things. Did Julian herself do that? No doubt she often did. Indeed at times it would have been important for her to eliminate, not only some, but even every thought if she were to become in prayer united with the totally transcendent One who, then, could somehow flow though her to touch the lives of others whom she knew. But, if in leaving for a while those thoughts which worry us, we all are able to discover inner freedom, that does not explain how all things can be well. And Julian herself must have been conscious of that, too.

The second way she tried to solve this problem was to posit some 'great deed' which was, and still is, to be done. That seemed to her to be what we might call a 'theological conclusion'. She, in any case, was sure that God could do all things and that he wanted everybody to be saved and so, it seemed that, in his wisdom, he must have some way of bringing all that is into his everlasting life. Of course, she did not know what that 'great deed' would be nor did she know how it was going to be done. However, she was sure, that some day, somehow, it would happen and that, when it did, all would indeed be well. Beyond that intuition her exploring mind could see no more and yet the thought that there was more to be revealed allowed her to relax and to continue in her chosen way of life. At least a door for everyone, including those who had already died, was open and she could continue telling those who came to her that God, who does not see things as we see them, could, through that great final deed, fulfil his own intentions and make all things very well.[19]

Julian, of course, was grappling with a great dilemma which in different ways is able to confuse us all. In her case, since she was convinced that God is good and loving, it must have been very difficult to see how anything or anyone could not be good and quite impossible to understand how anybody could be lost. Indeed such pessimistic thoughts did not fit easily into her way of thinking and, at times, she must have wondered if they fitted into God's! But, on the other hand, she must have realised that those who never knew the touch of love in their own lives can find it difficult to put their trust in One who is, as she herself believed, all-love. It, consequently, must have been for their sake, and not only for her own, that she continued to do all she could to treasure and to nurture her own deep conviction: that, in spite of all the counter-signs, God loves us with a love which is, not only infinite, but infinitely powerful too.

It is fitting to God's royal dominion to keep his privy counsel in peace and it is fitting to his servants out of obedience and respect not to wish to know his counsel. (LT 30)	It is the glory of God to conceal things. (Prov 25:5)
There is a deed which the Blessed Trinity will perform on the last day, as I see it, … in this deed he will preserve his word in everything. And he will make well all which is not well. (LT 32)	O the depth of the riches and knowledge of God! How unsearchable are his judgements and how inscrutable his ways! For from him and through him and to him are all things. (Rom 11:33-36)

THE THIRST

Perhaps, it would be good to pause here for a moment to reflect on one particular detail which attracted Julian at this stage in her 'great experience'. It was a detail which suggested something more profound than what it primarily meant. Moreover, it was one which, staying somewhere in her mind, may have begun to

merge with images which she would only later find and so become surprisingly enriched. We will have to consider some of
those. But first let us direct our gaze to that initial detail which so
fascinated Julian: the thirst which Christ endured as he lay
dying on the cross.

There was, as Julian saw very well, an urgency about that
thirst. It was no mild desire to have an appetising or refreshing
drink, but one which in the scriptures had already been associated
with that agonising moment when his dehydrated body was
about to die. His yearning and his need, in other words, were
great. His thirst, indeed, seemed to express to Julian the craving
of his total being. Moreover, it was one which was for something
which, she could perceive, included her!

The physical desire of Christ which was for water as he hung
upon the cross would, certainly, have been extreme. However,
that desire, as seen by Julian in her own 'great experience', was
symbolising something more important and more relevant to
her. What that was had already been suggested by St John when
in his gospel he had spoken of the time when Jesus asked a
woman in Samaria to offer him a drink. That drink which he desired was obviously more than just a cup of water from a well. It
was no other than that sinful woman's confidence and faith.

That spiritualising way of understanding scripture was quite
common in the Middle Ages, thanks to St Augustine[20] and to
others whose reflections on the sacred text were known. It,
therefore, could have been through preachers of the period or
maybe through some scholars who had helped her to explain
her own experience that Julian first heard of this interpretation
of the thirst of Christ which she so willingly accepted as her
own. Did it not illustrate and reinforce for her her own belief
that, like that woman in Samaria, she was herself the special ob-
ject of the Lord's desire?

At first, it was indeed most probably herself whom she considered as the favoured one. But later, as her spiritual life ma-
tured, she much more easily included in her thinking the extended truth that Christ desired all other people too. In doing so,
she would, no doubt, have thought especially of people whom

she knew and whom, perhaps, in some way she had tried to help but afterwards she seems to have included everyone. Within that universally inclusive thought, it was of course quite clear to Julian that that great thirst which she had seen in Christ could not be satisfied until the end of time, until that great deed which she was expecting had itself been done, until that last soul to be saved was actually saved. That thirst, which was itself divine, was for them all.

This later insight was, however, linked to and, indeed, to some extent dependent on another which she was to have a little after that. This other insight was that the divine desire came, ultimately, not from him who gave his life for her, but from the loving Father of us all. In consequence the role of Christ would seem to be, not just of loving her, but also of assisting everyone, including her, to grow into what she could call the fruit, or fruits, for which the Father thirsted and which, when prepared, he would most willingly receive. That was a graphic and, indeed, perhaps a eucharistic[21] thought, though one which ripened only after she had come to understand her enigmatic picture-parable. But when it did, it could be said to have enriched her early thought about the thirst of Christ by putting it within a context which was greater and more universally involving. It was, consequently, one in which her visitors and friends could find how precious were their own lives to the One who wants to bring us all beyond the cross into that life which, while absorbing us, is able to fulfil our deepest aspirations too.

This is Christ's spiritual thirst, his longing in love which persists and always will until we see him on the day of judgement. (LT 31)	Jesus said to the woman: 'Give me to drink. (Jn 4:7)
This is his thirst and his longing in love for us, to gather us all into him, to our endless joy, as I see it. (LT 31)	Jesus, knowing that all was finished, said: 'I thirst'. (Jn 19:28)

There was a treasure in the earth which the Lord loved. It is a food which is pleasing and delicious to the Lord. The servant was to work and make sweet streams to run and fine and plenteous fruit to grow, which he was to bring before the Lord. (LT 51)

God wants everyone to be saved and to reach full knowledge of the truth. (1 Tim 2:3)

Christ, the first-fruits, then those who belong to him. Then he delivers the kingdom to God the Father. (cf. 1 Cor 15:23-24)

SIN WILL BE NO SHAME

It took a while before she noticed it. But it was there: a feeling in herself that she would sin! Perhaps, that was because, inadequate before the love which she perceived in Christ, she knew how easy it would be for her to opt for something much more manageable for herself and, maybe, for a lot of other people too. In any case, it seemed to her that she might for a moment disregard that all-consuming love and, settling for some less demanding possibility, behave in some way which would later cause her shame. She shivered at the very thought. But, even as she did, she knew that, if and when that moment came, the One who loved her would protect her and she, consequently, was consoled and able to relax.

As Julian reflected later on that weakness which she noticed in herself, a thought which put it in perspective came into her mind. It was that, even if some sin should be a cause of shame for her, or any other person, shame itself would not have to remain but could eventually disappear. That could occur, she realised, because when all will be revealed all those who will be saved will see the love in which they had been guided all the time. They would, in other words, perceive that any sin which previously had made them ashamed was, in the eyes of God, no more than just a stage on their own journey into him. In that perspective shame itself will vanish in a sense of universal gratitude. But Julian could also see that in some cases that already was occurring even then.

Julian, it seems, enjoyed reflecting on this latter fact and in explaining it with illustrations from the lives of well-known people too. Thus she would speak about King David who, although he had sinned grievously, became an honoured person, not just for the people of his time but also for the generations which were yet to come. She also spoke of Peter who, despite his momentary lack of trust (which she as we have seen could understand)[22] was to become accepted by the church as one of its outstanding saints. Then there were Paul and Mary Magdalen and John of Beverley,[23] that Englishman who once had seriously sinned but who at her time was accepted by a lot of people as a neighbour who, to use her own word here, had been exceptionally 'kind'. In him and in those others whom she spoke about some inextinguishable spark had grown into a flame. In each the inner and the stronger part, which is as we have noted in us all, had tamed the outer, wayward one[24] and so, despite their shameful past, their sin no longer is a barrier in their relationship with God. Indeed, while they were still on earth it had begun to have a positive effect: it had allowed them to discover just how much they needed help and, probably, to reach out with compassion to a lot of other people who were struggling on their way.

This was in fact the road which Julian travelled too. No doubt there were a number of occasions when it seemed to her that she had sinned but only to discover that the Lord was guiding her through those events in order to enjoy an even greater unity with him. That, certainly, would seem to be what happened in that interval between the main part of her 'great experience' and the short part which was still to come. Apparently, she told a visitor who called to see her that she had been only raving and, in doing so, denied the value of the revelations which she had received. A little later, thanks to that same visitor, she realised her fault and was, as she admits, ashamed.[25] But, as the rest of her own life suggests, that lapse or sin turned out to be a door for many blessings too. It helped her to appreciate how fragile is the life of faith and, consequently, to do all she could to benefit from all that it is able to bestow.

In this connection, let us link those sinner saints with that mysterious 'servant' of the picture-parable which baffled her at first. He too was one who had in some way fallen down into a situation from which by himself he could not rise. But he, like all those other saints, had also been raised up. Indeed, he was exalted to a place beside the loving Father of us all.[26] If, Julian, still unaware of who he really was, did not explicitly associate him with those other saints when she was naming them, she did make one remark which was indicative of insights yet to come. It was that God, who loves us even in our weakness and our sins, sees all of us as if we were but one.[27] The picture-parable, when fully understood, would make it clear to her who that one really is and, therefore, why, in spite of any sins which may have worried us, we have good reason to believe that we are fundamentally secure.

God showed that sin will be no shame. (LT 38)

Happy the man whose offence is forgiven (Ps 31/32)

Just as various sins are punished with various pains, so will they be rewarded with various joys in heaven to reward the victories over them. (LT 38)

'Come, let us reason together', says the Lord: though your sins are like scarlet, they shall be as white as snow. (Is 1:18)

God brought joyfully to my mind David and inumerable others... Magdalen, Peter and Paul... and others too without number; how they and their sins are known to the church on earth and this is no shame to them, but everthing is turned to honour (LT 38)

But the father said to servants: Bring quickly the best robe and put it on him; and put a ring on his hand and shoes on his feet; and bring the fatted calf and let us eat and make merry; for this, my son, was dead and is alive again; he was lost and is found And they began to make merry. (Lk 15:22-24)

THE HEALING PROCESS

While Julian was certain that all would be well, she was aware that, on the human level, there are stages through which we must go for that to be attained. She, therefore, spoke, not only of the healing love of God, but also of the different ways in which we must co-operate with him if we are to become completely cured. What she wrote in her book concerning this was certainly the consequence of her own 'great experience' but it, no doubt, was also the result of listening to a lot of people who were wounded by the circumstances and decisions of their lives.

The Scourge

'Sin will be no shame' said Julian to many of those people but she was aware that, long before the happy day when that would be the case, sin often is a scourge. A scourge! One wonders if there had been times when Julian had seen a public flogging or had cause to ponder its immediate effects. In any case, a number of those people who had come to her appear to have been very broken or, to use her own words, to have felt 'not fit for anything at all'. Today, we possibly would speak about a loss of self-esteem or of the way that life can take a downward course and go from bad to worse but Julian just spoke of certain people as not feeling fit for anything except to sink down, as it were, to hell. Yet those same people were, she knew, her 'even-Christians' and her role was, therefore, to receive them kindly and to help them find some reason to believe that much could still be well. She, therefore, would have tried to tell them, by her attitude if not by words, that sinking feelings did not mean that God himself had let them down or that he did not have a great desire to lift them up – on high.

Contrition

Contrition was, not just a most important, but a central element for Julian in her own understanding of our lives. The word itself, it could be noted here, comes from a Latin root suggesting something 'ground down', as a grain of corn can be, but what had to be 'ground down' at this stage for Julian were elements such as the 'vain affections' and the 'pride' (exaggerated self-esteem?) which she found even in herself. However, if I may adapt this metaphor, it could be said that as the breaking of the husk allows the corn itself to grow so too the breaking of such obstacles is able to allow our true selves to develop as they should. Expressing that in Julian's terms, we could declare that, when the 'outer part' of us, so prone to its own independent growth, is crushed by our acceptance of the trials and disappointments of this life, we have a special moment in which we may find again our deeper and our 'inner part' and, consequently, offer it another opportunity to grow. This process may, of course, be quite a painful one but it is able to release our true selves for the happiness for which we have been made.

Hope & Healing

As inner life begins to grow, a sense of hope begins to blossom too. Our anchoress may have observed this taking place in some of those who came to her for help, especially if they were people who returned from time to time. In fact, her very patient hearing of their sorrows may have helped a lot of them to feel less broken in themselves and so to glimpse, and then receive, the first rays of a growing and transforming light. Who knows how many may have even felt, as they developed a relationship with Julian: 'if she is able to accept me as I am, perhaps God will accept me too'? But Julian may have experienced this same kind of refreshing hope within herself as well. She may, for instance, after 'feeling low' or even, for some reason, 'foul', have found that in her quiet-time the presence of the loving God was somehow cleansing her and guaranteeing, through a growing sense of peace, that in the end all can indeed be well.

Confession

Confession was for Julian, it should be noted, not the first step on that road which leads to health, but one within a process which already had begun. That was perhaps a deeper understanding of it than is often shown but, more importantly for us, it is an understanding which reflects our own experience as

well. Do we not often need some time to think before we can express to someone else the deeper movements of the heart? Do
we not need some time to realise that God has not stopped loving us before we can with confidence confess to anyone those
elements within our lives which have not yet been healed? Of
course, when Julian was speaking in this chapter of 'confession'
she was thinking of the sacramental practice of the church and,
as an anchoress, she probably would have confessed her own
sins and her failings to some spiritual father, even once a week.
However, since she has confessed some faults and weaknesses
to us, the readers of her book, there is no reason to suppose that
she did not accept the value of confession in a wider sense as
well.

Penance

As Julian was conscious that 'confession' could not be the first
step on the road to full recovery, so she was sure that it was not
the last. Indeed, the very giving of a 'penance' in the sacramental
practice of the church suggested that there was at least one other
step to come. However, while she noted that there was this special 'penance' to be done, she knew that there were many other
penances which had to be accepted too.[28] They would have been
those penances which come with life itself and which can range
from all the ordinary disappointments of each day to sicknesses
which come from time to time and, then, to those particularly
painful ones which are occasioned by some person's careless or
malicious word. It is, she knew, in our accepting all of these with
patience and with trust that healing can continue in our lives
and our capacity to welcome and enjoy the life which is to come
can grow.[29]

The Work of God

The more we ponder how to cope with sin with Julian as guide
the more we come to see that the most vital element in all of this
is not what we are doing (like 'confessing' and 'accepting
penances') but all that God himself is doing in and through us
all the time. Indeed, as Julian assures us, it is only in the context

of a faith and love relationship with God, which is itself a gift, that we can recognise our sins for what they really are[30] and, then, decide to take the necessary steps to reach that unity with him which we desire. To put that in a way more Trinitarian, we could say that as we go through the pains of true contrition and confession[31] and then do whatever penance is required, it is the Spirit of the loving Father which is leading us and, thereby, guiding us to him. Moreover, we could say that, as we let an inner peace begin to grow within ourselves, we have a sign that healing is already taking place and even that we are being moulded by the Spirit into Christ, with whom the Father is well pleased. Of course, the total healing which we need will not take place before the 'great deed' to be done is fully done.[32] However, in that deep, significant peace which we are able to experience and in the love which we who are in Christ are also able to receive, we have its first instalments and it guarantee.

Sin is the sharpest scourge with which any chosen soul can be struck, which scourge belabours man or woman, and breaks a man in his own sight so much that at times he thinks himself not fit for anything but as it were to sink into hell. (LT 39)

My guilt towers higher than my head; it is a weight too heavy to bear. My wounds are foul and festering; the result of my own folly. I am bowed and brought to my knees. I go mourning all day long. (Ps 37/38)

Contrition seizes him by the inspiration of the Holy Spirit and turns bitterness into hope. (LT 39)

And the Lord turned and looked at Peter. And Peter remembered the word of the Lord, how he had said to him, 'Before the cock crows today you will deny me three times'. And he went out and wept bitterly. (Lk 22:61-62)

Then the wounds begin to heal and the soul to revive. (LT 39)

Jesus took the blind man by the hand and led him out of the village; and when he had laid his hands on him, he asked him: 'do you see any-thing?' He looked up and said: 'I see men, but they look like trees walking.' Then Jesus laid his hands on his eyes again. (Mk 8:22-25)

The Holy Spirit leads him to confession, willing to reveal his sins, nakedly and truth-fully. (LT 39)

I kept it a secret and my frame was wasted, I groaned all day long ... But now I have ac-knowledged my sins: my guilt I did not hide. I said 'I will confess my offence to the Lord' and you Lord have forgiven the guilt of my sin (Ps 31/32)

Then he accepts the penance imposed for every sin... and bodily sickness sent by God and sorrows and outward shames with reproofs and contempt of the world and with all kinds of affliction and temptation into which we are cast, spiritually and bodily. (LT 39)

We rejoice in our sufferings, knowing that suffering pro-duces endurance, and en-durance produces character, and character produces hope, and hope does not disappoint us, because God's love has been poured into our hearts through the Holy Spirit which has been given to us. (Rom 5:3-5)

No more than God's love for us is withdrawn because of our sin, does he wish our love to be withdrawn from our-selves or from our 'even-Christians'. (LT 40)

Beloved, let us love one an-other, for love is of God and he who loves is born of God... for God is love. (1 Jn 4:7-8)

Love your neighbour as your-self. (Mt 22:39)

Notes

1. cf. ST chapter 8 & LT chapter 11
2. cf. LT chapter 73
3. To think of suffering as sent by God as punishment for sin could lead, not only to contrition, but to many kinds of penitential acts as well. In this connection, one could note the Flagellant Movement which had spread through Europe when the Plague and other great disasters had occurred. The Flagellants indulged in organised self-scourging and, although they were not strong in England, the remark of Julian that she did not have any insights on the value of self-chosen penances (cf. LT chapter 77) suggests that there were people whom she knew who hoped that God might be appeased by those which they performed.
4. Julian wrote about herself: 'it would be most unkind of me to blame God since he does not blame me at all'. It was important for her to transcend those useless and unanswerable questions which the mind inevitably asks and to resist the urge to use God as a scapegoat for the sufferings we do not like.
5. Her faith convinced her that all would be well. However, it is interesting to note that she was sure that at the end of time we all will see the reason for so many things which are confusing to us now. Then 'we shall all say with one voice: "Lord, blessed may you be; because it is so, it is well".' (LT 85)
6. In the famous picture-parable about a servant and a lord, the servant fell into a dell, a hollow in the ground. That empty space appears to be an image of the emptiness of sin. (cf. LT chapter 51)That is an interesting corollary to the thought that sin is nothing, which is offered to us in the Short Text, chapter 8.
7. cf. ST chapter 8 & LT chapter 12.
8. Julian referred explicitly to the 'image' when she wrote that it is soiled by sin. (ST chapter 17 & LT chapter 39). Much later, when she spoke of Christ as Mother, she implied it when she wrote that he can clean us when we have become 'filthy and unlike him'. (LT chapter 61). The phrase she uses here would seem to echo that of Genesis, chapter 1 which said that humankind is made 'in the image and likeness of God'
9. Urban V1, the Roman claimant, was supported by the Bishop of Norwich, Henry Despenser, against the claims of Clement who had been supported by the French.
10. cf. 'Holy Church will be shaken in sorrow and anguish and tribulation in this world as men shake a cloth in the wind'. While Julian would seem to be considering the future here, she may be also saying that, because the church is in this world, it is inevitably in a suffering and a struggling state.
11. This does not mean that Julian would not have sympathised with

many of the criticisms which some others made. Indeed, the fact that she considered that she might have sinned through pride (ST 13), as well as her insistence on her loyalty suggests that she may have been tempted to condemn a lot of what was happening at the time. However, her preferred and chosen way was to accept the church with all its imperfections and to let the love of God change her and all her 'even-Christians' from within.

12. cf. LT chapter 19.

13. In the Long Text, Julian had already spoken of the body of the Crucified as 'torn in pieces like a cloth' and, in a later paragraph,as 'hanging in the air, as people hang up a cloth to dry'. (LT chapter 17)

14. cf. LT chapter 28.

15. cf. LT chapter 51 (last paragraph).

16. Julian had a probing mind. Although she realised that there were limits to what she could understand, she struggled to discover some solution to the problems raised by her conviction that all will be well. It is, perhaps, amusing and says much about her character that, while believing that she should relax and put her trust in God, her mind was always ready to explore a little more the mysteries of faith.

17. While the official teaching of the church is that damnation is a possibility, it has not ever been declared that any individual has been eternally condemned.

18. cf. two verses of scripture: 'Blot them out from the book of the living' (Ps 68/69:29) and 'if anyone's name is not found in the book of life, he was thrown into the lake of fire' (Rev 20:15).

19. Although she did not say so in this chapter, Julian may have associated this 'great deed' which will be done at the end of time with the transformation of the servant in the picture-parable of chapter 51. In other words, it can be thought of in connection with the Resurrection which, when it has fully taken place, will show so much to be so different to what it now appears to be.

20. St Augustine, one of the most influential authors of the Middle Ages wrote: 'he, who was seeking a drink, was searching of that woman's faith'. (Tractate in John, 15)

21. There is a certain eucharistic note in Julian as she speaks of the food and drink which is to be prepared and offered to the Lord by his devoted and self-sacrificing servant. We read: 'The servant was to take this food and drink and carry it most worshipfully before the lord'. (cf. LT chapter 51)

22. cf. ST chapter 9 & LT chapter 15.

23. John of Beverley (Yorkshire) was bishop of Hexhan (c.687-705), then of York (705-717). After retiring from that see, he withdrew to a reli-

gious house in Beverley, which he had founded, and died there in 721. Miracles were attributed to his intercession and his tomb became a place for pilgrimage. As for the 'serious sin' which he is said to have committed (and which Julian presumes to have been public knowledge), there is no further evidence available today.

24. cf. LT chapter 19.

25. cf. ST chapter 21 & LT chapter 66.

26. cf. LT chapter 51.

27. 'God loves all who will be saved, all of them as if they were but one soul' (LT chapter 38. cf. ST chapter 17).

28. cf. LT chapter 77.

29. The Ritual for Sacramental Absolution recognises the connection which exists between these different penances. 'May the Passion of our Lord Jesus Christ, whatever good you do and sufferings you endure heal your sins, help you to grow in holiness.'

30. cf. LT chapter 78.

31 cf. ST chapter 17 & LT chapter 40.

32. cf. LT chapter 32.

Part Four

Prayer

The willing servant and his loving Lord

In her 14th 'Showing' Julian saw something of the nature and the power of prayer. However, since her commentary on this within her second book is longer than what she had written in her first, we must conclude that there were many details which she only later came to understand. In fact, the longer text itself admits that that was so.

I am including in this fourth part of my own book one small section which in fact refers to what the following, or 15th, 'Showing' showed. It was the final answer to, and so the ultimate fulfilment of, our fundamental yearning and our prayer.

The nucleus of Julian's own understanding of the nature and the power of prayer revolved around three points: that true prayer is inspired, that we experience our prayer in different ways and that there is a 'quiet prayer' which everybody can enjoy.

We are concerned with chapter 19 in the Short Text and with chapters 41-43 in the extended, longer text.

INFALLIBLE PRAYER

Julian within her 'great experience' perceived a humbling yet empowering fact. It was that her own prayer was part of something which was greater and more powerful than herself. It was no less than part of that great flow of energy which comes from God and then, involving all of us in different ways, can carry us on its return to him.

The consequence of such an insight was that Julian began to see more clearly that her role, while certainly important, was a secondary and subsidiary one. Indeed, at times it may have been no more than just to recognise and to accept that fundamental yearning[1] which was in her as she went about her ordinary tasks. At other times, of course, it would have been much more. It would have been to focus all her thoughts in the direction of the One her fundamental yearning sought so that that very yearning could express itself in active longing and in words of gratitude if not of marvelling delight.[2] Those would have been the moments of her more explicit prayer. However in both cases she was sure that, if she did not hinder in some way that mighty current of divine desire, it would bring her inevitably towards its ever-satisfying source.

104

As Julian continued to reflect on her own prayer, she came to see the Trinitarian dimensions which its exercise implied. At first, as indicated in her shorter text, she had considered it within the context of a love relationship with Christ. His very presence had appeared to her to be, to use her own word here, the 'ground' from which her wanting and beseeching grew. That wanting and beseeching were, in consequence, for him and for an ever-growing unity between them which, she knew, was what he wanted too. However, while that understanding of her prayer remained, she came to see it, as I intimated, as a part of something which was greater and in fact much more fulfiling too.

It was when she began to think of Christ, not just as one who loved her, but as someone who was, as it were, on her side that she came to see more clearly that her prayer, and those of everybody else as well, were ultimately to the Father of us all. The role of Christ was, consequently, seen by her in two distinct but complementary ways. At times he seemed to be the first recipient of her own Spirit-generated prayer but ever ready, as it were, 'to send it up above'.[3] At other times he seemed to be the one with whom she merged in one great act of yearning for an ever-deeper union with the One from whom we all have come. In either case, the strong flow of the Spirit carried her, as it can carry everyone, to Christ, the well-beloved Son, and then, with him, into the very source of rich and everlasting life.

This flow of energy, as Julian perceived, is very, very great. Yet, as she noticed too, it cannot carry us towards its ever-overflowing source until our own prayer has acquired two predisposing and essential qualities. The first is that it should be 'rightful' and the second that it should be full of confidence and trust and both, she realised, came from that energising Spirit too.

That prayer be 'rightful' means, according to the explanation in her shorter book, that it is for those very gifts, or for the one essential gift, which God desires to give.[4] 'A bit unsatisfactory', one could easily complain. However, when one realises that to want what God himself desires to give us is to want that very grace for which we have in fact been made, the situation should

not seem so bad! Indeed, as Julian knew very well,[5] to pray to
God for anything of less importance would be to request from
him a gift which would not ever fully satisfy. Such prayer could
hardly be considered absolutely 'right'.

But did not Julian herself pray frequently about a lot of ordinary things? No doubt she did. Indeed, it could be said that,
since she was convinced that God is interested in all the small
events of life[6] as well as in the greater ones, she would most
probably have prayed about the needs and the events of every
day. However, we could also say that prayer which is connected
with such ordinary things is *prayer about* those very things which
can in some way help us on our journey through this world.
What Julian continued *praying for*, however, would have been
that constantly increasing oneness with the One who loved her[7]
which can take place in this present life as well as in the next.
That would have been, indeed, a very 'rightful' prayer and one,
moreover, which we, certainly could think of as especially inspired.

The second of the two conditions which must be fulfiled before we can be carried on towards the fullness of the love we
seek is that our trusting never fails. We have already noted that
to trust in God is in itself a very valuable gift, especially when
life does not seem to be going in the way that we had hoped.[8]
But now, as Julian reflected on her own experience in prayer, she
realised how absolutely, if not crucially, important such a trust
can be. To keep the flowing metaphor, she realised that it is only
trust which will allow us to let go of all those things upon the
river-bank of life which can so easily entangle us and thereby
hold us back. Indeed, she may have also realised that frequently
we have to make an act of faith that there will even be a central
current to convey us as we keep on yearning for an all-absorbing
and completely satisfying sea.

It should be noted that, while Julian was conscious of the different situations in which people find themselves, she never
spoke of 'making progress' nor did she suggest that there is any
need to think of doing so. She was too conscious of the fact that
people have to keep on coping with the same kind of reality

from one day to the next. Just as one corner in a winding river may appear to any item flowing with it much like those which had been met before, so too the obstacles which we find on our journey through this life may not be very different to those which have already faced us in the past. Yet, while our lives may seem at times to be composed of many similar stops and starts, there is, she also knew, not far from us a constant, if a hidden, movement of the Spirit as it flows from the eternal Father to and through the Son and then returns to him. Good living on our part is, therefore, to allow that Spirit flow through us as well and prayer is both to wish that it will keep on doing so and to rejoice because it actually does.

And our Lord said: 'I am the ground of your beseeching. First it is my will that you should have it and then I make you to wish it and then I make you to beseech it. If I make you beseech it, how could it be that you would not have what you beseech? (LT 41)

Apart from me you can to nothing. (Jn 15:5)

He who searches the hearts of all knows what is the mind of the Spirit, because the Spirit intercedes for the saints according to the will of God. (Rom 8:27)

Beseeching is a true, enduring will of the soul, united and joined to our Lord's will by the sweet, secret operation of the Holy Spirit. (LT 41)

When the Spirit of truth comes, he will guide you into all truth. (Jn 16:13)

Whatever you ask the Father in my name, he will give it to you. (Jn 15:17)

Prayer unites the soul to God... Prayer makes the soul like God when the soul wills as God wills; then it is like God in condition, as it is in nature. (ST 19)

As Jesus prayed, the aspect of his face was changed. (Lk 9:29)

PLAYING OUR PART

'I am sure', wrote Julian, 'that no one asks, or prays, for mercy or for grace, unless that mercy and that grace has been already given'. A profoundly theological remark! However, to receive the mercy and the grace of God implies that, in his Spirit, God has been already working in our lives and so when we are pray-ing for the Holy Spirit, we have reason to be sure that it has also been, to some extent at least, both given and received. In fact, while we are actually asking for it, it is guiding our desires. Our prayer in other words is always, as we noted, part of one great movement which begins before our contribution to it has been made. But both the statement made by Julian and my suggested version of it can imply a complementary truth: that, even if our contribution is a secondary one, it is important too. Indeed, it is essential. God who wants to do so much for us can do so only if we make the effort to co-operate with him.

It is, however, in co-operating with him that we often fail. Indeed, when Julian referred to people who desired to have some kind of mediator for their prayer,[9] she seems to have con-sidered them as lacking in the confidence which they had reason to possess. Some of those very people may in fact have come to Julian herself and, having poured out all their worries, they may have petitioned her to pray that they would get what they de-sired. However, while no doubt she often did, she would, it seems to me, have also tried to help them to believe that God is always kind and welcoming and, therefore, that they could with confidence approach him for themselves. In other words, al-though she realised that people can support each other in their prayers,[10] she would have intimated that it has to be through each one's own desiring prayer that God is able to fulfil their deepest yearnings, and indeed his own.

One can, perhaps, imagine people at her anchorhold com-plaining that, while they themselves did not neglect to pray, they did not feel that doing so was helping them at all. In such a situation, Julian no doubt would have been understanding and, to help, she may at times have even spoken of the moments in her own life when she felt that prayer was almost pointless and of how she, consequently, coped. But there must have been other times when she would have suggested to those very people that, perhaps, what they were asking God to give them was not really what they needed most. Indeed, she may have added that the very reason why their prayers remained unanswered could have been because there was 'a better gift' which God desired to give them and for which they had not yet begun to pray. She would, of course, have wanted them both to discern the nature of that 'better gift' and, then, to keep on praying for it too. Although it might not be immediately given (that she knew) to keep on praying for it would at least dispose them to receive it when the moment for its coming would arrive.

If Julian herself had barren moments in her prayer,[11] she obviously persevered. She even 'worked in prayer', to use one of her own expressions here. While that would have implied remaining faithful to some periods of time each day when she could put all else aside, it would have also meant facilitating those particularly sacred moments by reflecting frequently on all that God had previously done. But, if she 'worked in prayer' in that and other ways, and so allowed the yearning in herself to grow, she worked in what she called 'good living' too. What that would have implied for someone living in a anchorhold we can but guess. However, to recall a metaphor, we could suggest that she did all that she could to stop her 'outer part' from being caught in any of those suffocating weeds which always grow along the river bank of life. In less poetic words, she must have coped with all the details of her ordinary daily life in such a way that none of them became an obstacle to her relationship with God. What always mattered most was that her spirit would be absolutely free for him who made her for himself and who, of course, would be for her the greatest gift of all.

As Julian continued in her own relationship with God, she came to realise how powerful and how useful was the 'word' which she had heard. That 'word' was in a very special way the one she had received in her own 'great experience' and which she frequently recalled. It was a 'word', however, which was similar in meaning to the one which had been given through the scriptures and which echoed through the liturgies which formed the framework for the church's daily prayer. Indeed, for Julian herself it may have echoed also through the books which she possessed or which she heard some dedicated mentor read. However, it was when she pondered that life-giving 'word' in private, that she realised how useful it could actually be. To paraphrase her own words here, it could ignite and warm her heart so that, with its continued help, she would be able to respond more lovingly to him from whom it had, of course, originally come.

The passage in the longer text of Julian which speaks of this explicitly is very short but, nonetheless, it is a precious and a valuable one. Indeed, for all who like to read and ponder scripture and to let its thoughts guide their own yearnings it assures them that the Word of God is full of a transforming power. For those, who wish to concentrate on certain verses for a while, it can assure them that their meaning, or the Word within the words they read or memorise, is worthy of the effort to receive it which they make. To be precise, while they are making every effort to continue to accept that Word into their daily lives, it can do more than merely help them. It can quietly absorb them into its own vitalising life. It can, moreover, quietly transform them more and more into the One who is himself that Word Personified. Perhaps when Julian perceived the meaning of her famous picture-parable she also glimpsed what I am saying here. In any case she saw that it is through allowing him, whom scripture also calls the Word, to enter into us that we are able to become united to the One whose Word it ultimately is.

As Julian allowed this Word to guide her and to mould her, she became aware of movements of deep gratitude within her prayer. Although she knew that she had not yet reached the fullness of that joy for which she had been made, she also knew that there was so much which she had in fact been more than lucky to receive. The point of interest here, however, is that, when she spoke of gratitude, or of thanksgiving, in the context of her prayer she was referring, not to graces which she had been given in the past, though they were many, but to those which she was then receiving as she prayed. She was, it could be said, referring in a special way to that transforming Spirit which was at that very moment mingling with her own. Indeed that Spirit was already oneing her with Christ himself and, thereby, guaranteeing that, not just her feeble prayers, but she herself was very much accepted by the ever-loving and enfolding Father of us all.[12]

Pray wholeheartedly, though you may feel nothing, though you may see nothing, yes, though you think that you could not, for in dryness and barrenness, in sickness and in weakness, then is your prayer most pleasing to me, though you think it almost tasteless to you. (LT 41)

Rejoice in your hope, be patient in tribulation, be constant in prayer. (Rom 12:12)

The Lord delights in those who revere him, in those who wait for his love. (Ps 147)

I am sure, according to our Lord's meaning, that either we are waiting for a better occasion or more grace or a better gift. (LT 42)

What no eye has seen, nor ear heard, nor the heart of man conceived, what God has prepared for those who love him. (1 Cor 2:9)

Reason and grace drive the soul to implore the Lord with words, recounting his blessed Passion. And so the Power of the Lord's word enters the soul and enlivens the heart and it begins by his grace faithful exercise, and makes the soul to pray most blessedly and truly to rejoice in our Lord. (LT 41)

For as the rain and the snow come down from heaven and return not thither but water the earth, making it bring forth and sprout, giving seed to the sower and bread to the eater, so shall my word be that goes forth from my mouth; it shall not return to me empty but it shall accomplish that which I purpose, and prosper in the thing for which I sent it. (Is 55:10-11)

With thanksgiving, we ought to pray for the deed which is now being done. (LT 42)	By prayer and supplication with thanksgiving, let your requests be made known to God. (Phil 4:6)

QUIET PRAYER

Julian must have had a lot of quiet moments in her day. 'Quiet' in the sense that she was undisturbed by visitors and quiet in the sense that she was sometimes undisturbed by even the demands of thought. Such moments must have been refreshing ones, especially perhaps if she had been exposed to many of the worrying concerns of other people's lives. But were those moments only periods in which the tensions of the day began to fade or were they also sacred times in which some part of her was quietly engaged in prayer? That is, no doubt, a question which she was not ever asked but it is, certainly, the kind of question which a lot of people who become involved in quiet-prayer groups tend to ask today. When they have spent a half an hour in restful silence they can say that it was both a calming and enjoyable experience yet they can also, with some hesitation, ask: 'but was it really prayer?' The fact that they were not addressing words to God nor even thinking thoughts about him seems quite often to suggest that what was happening could not be described in such a way. Yet prayer, which certainly can be expressed in words and thoughts, comes from that part of us which lies beneath them both. What many people in a quiet-prayer group can experience is, therefore, no less than the early symptoms of what is, in fact, a deep and very valuable form of prayer.

However it would hardly be correct to think of Julian herself as moving without any problem into inner silence every time she settled down for prayer. Instead, she may have frequently at such a moment been distracted by the memories of happenings which had in some way worried or excited her, and maybe only just a little while before. Yet, on the other hand, when she had coped with all her many thoughts and, as it were, had filed them, she would then have let herself become more conscious of that unseen presence which is indefinable because it is itself divine. Some writers,[13] let us note, will say that, since that presence is 'no-thing' (or nothing!), we should make an effort to reject our thoughts in order to unite with him who is above them all. But Julian prefers to lead us by a gentler, if no less demanding, route. She has already said that all the goodness which she found in everything is God[14] and so it seems that she would have us find that goodness which, while all around us, is especially revealed through Christ and, then, to let it lead us in its own way to its ever-overflowing source.

It is when that occurs that one prays in a way which is beyond the need for any word, or any thought and which, indeed, may not be even recognised to be a prayer at all until its quiet and refreshing moments have already passed. However Julian, who recognised the imperceptibility of such a satisfying prayer, assures us that in some way it can also overflow at times into our 'outer part', which she can call our 'sensuality', and there of course its presence will be much more easily perceived. Yet sensual phenomena can come from many causes, as most people know today, and so perhaps it was with wisdom that when Julian referred to what tradition calls our 'spiritual senses'[15] it was only in connection with the life that is to come. But, while she spoke of 'seeing', 'feeling', 'hearing' even 'smelling' God and 'tasting' him in heaven, it is clear that sometimes in her quiet prayer some of those future pleasures were, to some extent at least, already hers. Moreover, it would seem from what she wrote that she was sure that in their quiet prayer her 'even-Christians', and indeed all those for whom she wrote, could also find that rich experience of being in the presence of the all-surpassing yet all-loving One.

When Julian, in later life, reflected on such special moments in her own relationship with God she sometimes thought and spoke of them in ways which bordered on the matrimonial. She indicated, for example, that she had allowed herself to be completely captivated by the One who loved her and, within her second book, she even intimated that he had in many ways both stimulated and encouraged her desire.[16] Some theologians whom she may have known, may have been quite content to speak about such intimacies in an abstract and objective way. They could have used expressions like 'prevenient grace' or one which is 'concomitant' or even 'sanctifying'.[17] But the lady Julian preferred to speak from her own personal experience and to express herself in more affective terms. That does not mean that she was always living in a spiritual glow, or that her imperceptible prayer was always overflowing into her own 'sensuality', but it implies that she was sure that she herself was one with God in love and that she was convinced that such relationships can grow.

As Julian continued in her dedicated life, her trust in God who loved her may have been in some way strengthened as she came to focus on the trinitarian dimensions of his life. She had, of course, already realised that her own deepest prayer came ultimately, not from somewhere in herself, but from the very one whose love was drawing her to him. However, as she thought more deeply about God as Father, Son and Holy Spirit, she began to see more clearly that it is the Father who in his great love inspired her prayer as he inspires the prayers of everyone, and then becomes their ultimate and welcoming recipient. Within that context she was able then to see the most decisive reason why her prayer, and every prayer in which the Spirit of the Father flows, will be infallibly fulfilled. It is because they come from those who are substantially united to the second person of the Trinity, and so the Father can perceive in all who pray to him, however silently, the image[18] and the likeness of his own beloved Son. So Julian was able to relax and, in her quiet moments, to allow the life which is divine to flow, however imperceptibly, through hers.

When our courteous Lord of his special grace shows himself to our soul, we have what we desire.	I found him whom my soul loves; I held him and would not let him go. (Cant 3:4)

As I see it, this is an exalted and imperceptible prayer. (LT 43)

The kingdom of God is as if a man should scatter seed upon the ground... and the seed should sprout and grow and he knows not how. (Mk 4:26-27)

I saw that when we see the need to pray, then our Lord is following us, helping our desire. But when we, by his special grace, behold him plainly, seeing no other, we then necessarily follow him and he draws us to him by love. (LT 43)

My beloved speaks and says: 'Arise, my love, my fair one and come away.' (Cant 2:10)

Draw me after you, let us make haste. (Cant 1:4)

So we shall, by his sweet grace, come unto him by many secret touchings of sweet spiritual sights and feelings, measured out to us as our simplicity may bear it. (LT 43)

O that his left hand were under my head, and that his right hand embraced me! (Cant 2:6)

We shall all be endlessly hidden in God, truly seeing and wholly feeling, and hearing him spiritually and delectably smelling him and sweetly tasting him. (LT 43)

Now we see in a mirror dimly but then face to face. (1 Cor 13:12)

Taste and see that the Lord is good. (Ps 33/34)

'Behold, I will allure and speak tenderly to her.' (Hos 2:14)

Notes

1. cf. LT chapter 6

2. Frequently Julian used a short exclamation such as 'Blessed be God' and sometimes such an exclamation was a genuine expression of, apparently spontaneous delight.

3. It would be interesting to know how much the liturgy was an influence on Julian as she prayed. It could be noted here, at any rate, that prayer within the liturgy is normally addressed to God the Father, through the Son, and in the Holy Spirit.

4. cf. '(The first condition) is that they will not pray for anything at all but for the thing that is God's will and to his glory ' (ST chapter 19)

5. cf. The prayer which Julian herself composed and which she gives us in LT chapter 5.

6. 'For he wants us to know that the smallest thing will not be forgotten.' (cf. LT chapter 32)

7. cf. her prayer in LT chapter 5.

8. cf. LT chapter 10.

9. cf. LT chapter 6.

10. ibid.

11. 'Often we are as barren and dry after our prayer as we were before for I have experienced this myself. (LT chapter 41)

12. cf. LT chapter 51.

13. Such writers would include the author of the 'Cloud of Unknowing', a contemporary of Julian, who advocated putting all our thoughts beneath a cloud of forgetting.

14. cf. LT chapter 8.

15. From speaking of a 'spiritual sense', Origen began to speak of 'spiritual senses'. This idea was taken up by Gregory of Nyssa and, in the Middle Ages, it was echoed in the works of Bonaventure and some others of the Franciscan school. Sometimes these senses formed a kind of hierarchy: hearing the word, seeing its meaning, smelling or inhaling all its fragrance. Such a progress could then lead to the enjoyment of the taste of God and to the feel of his embrace. One notes that Julian, uninterested in this kind of progress-system, mentioned all five senses in a five-fold exposition of the rich delight which will be given in the world to come.

16. Note her reference to 'secret touchings' which 'will be done by the grace of the Holy Spirit, until the day that we die, still longing for love.' (LT chapter 43)

17. 'Prevenient grace' is the grace which comes to us before we act and makes it possible for us to do so. 'Concomitant grace' supports us in whatever we are doing. 'Sanctifying grace' affects our very being, being the result of God's own Spirit dwelling in us.

18. cf. LT chapter 51.

The second part of Julian's commentary on her 14th 'Showing' is, with very small exceptions, only in her second book. Moreover, much of it seems to belong, not to the first edition of that second book, but to a later one.

What we are to consider here explains why, when we have discovered 'rightful prayer', we can fulfil the second of the two conditions which have been proposed by Julian: 'to trust'. We can because, as Julian proclaims, there is no wrath in God, a fact which is itself connected with that other, deeper one: that as the Father looks at us he sees his own beloved Son. This leads her to reflect on this divine life which is in us and on how it can control and tame our 'outer part' while we allow ourselves to be embraced by it as if it were a loving mother and ourselves a growing child.

The passages in Julian's second book which now concern us are all found in chapters 45-63

No Wrath in God

'There is no wrath in God', said Julian to the people of her time. It was a startling statement since all suffering would have been considered as a sign that God was angry or annoyed. That was, it seemed, the obvious conclusion and especially when there were great afflictions to be borne. Indeed it is the one which is still possible today. Did not some people not too long ago declare that AIDS had been, not just allowed, but actually sent by God to be a punishment for sin? However Julian, and those who, consciously or not, were her own spiritual children, would not have agreed. They might have been content to say in such a case that 'maybe we had brought a punishment upon ourselves' but not that God himself was in a terrifying and vindictive rage.

There is no wrath in God. I had to lecture on that topic when, some years ago, I gave a course on Julian. However, I discovered that the startling nature of her statement, which of course I had to stress, had been accentuated by an unexpected headline in the media that day. Apparently, the gravestones in a cemetery had been quite badly vandalised and many people were upset and understandably annoyed. What had been emphasised, however, in one morning paper was the fact that, as a consequence, the local bishop had called down the wrath of God on those who had committed such a sacrilegious act. And I had to proclaim that very evening that there is no wrath in God at all!

I knew, as I began my talk, that all who had assembled would have seen or read the papers of that day and that they would have guessed that I had done the same. Not wanting to be too direct, I therefore let myself refer to situations in which people at the time of Julian would have had reason to become annoyed. I even mentioned in that context her aggressive bishop who had sent some social agitators to their death. He may, indeed, have been perceived by many of the Norwich people as the chosen instrument of a divine, avenging wrath and he, moreover, may have thought about himself in such a way. But, as I painted that kind of scenario it was to add that Julian, if she had had a chance to speak, might well have said with suitable politeness: 'Nay, my Lord; this wrath is not in God; it is within yourself!

Wrath was in fact perceived by Julian as the result of some lack in ourselves. If, for example, we do not possess the power to change some situation in the way that we would like, can we not feel annoyed and, if annoyance in us is intense, can we not show it in a violent or aggressive way? Or, if we do not know how to improve a situation which we do not like, can we not feel frustrated and, again, cannot that inner feeling manifest itself at times, not only in an angry way, but even quite destructively as well? Or, since there was in Julian a tendency to think in threes, we could speak also of a lack of goodness in ourselves and, consequently, of behaviour which is unacceptable. However, I do not suggest that human anger for whichever reason does not ever have a value in itself or that we should not use it in a proper way. I only say, with Julian, that we should not attribute it to God, whose nature is of course, not human, but divine.

I would submit that Julian's conviction that 'there is no wrath in God' is just as necessary in our own day as it was in hers. Indeed, there are a lot of people who have been brought up with the idea that God is some kind of a super-vigilant policeman, always ready to condemn the slightest fault and to impose some penalty as well. Although, one must admit, that there are many places even in the sacred scriptures which suggest the same, this image is a long way from the picture painted by St Luke: that of the Father who is totally unable not to welcome home his way-ward but repentant son.[1] That is, it always seems to me, one of the great climactic insights of the scriptural tradition and a high-point in God's revelation to us all. It certainly reveals the kind of God whom Julian was happy to proclaim: one who is always ready to enfold us in his un-extinguishable love.

An after-thought! It is that maybe we should re-examine how we understand the well-known, often-used expression: 'God forgives.' If it implies for us that God begins to pardon us when we, who have committed sin, have suitably repented then the God whom it is indicating would be one who is, not only changeable, but totally dependent on what we are doing for his attitude to us. It was, apparently, because of such a possible mis-understanding that, on one occasion, Julian declared that he does not forgive at all! Yet, at the same time, it is very clear that she was certain that he does forgive but in another and a better sense. It is that his *forgiving* is *for giving*, not just pardon for our sins, but also his own constant love which makes it possible for us to grow. Indeed it is that love which makes it possible for us, not only to repent of past mistakes, but to respond with confi-dence to him whose Spirit can both heal us where some healing is required and then dispose us so that we are able to receive it even more.

I understood that sinners sometimes deserve blame and wrath and I could not see these two in God. (LT 45)	His Father saw him and had compassion and ran and embraced him and kissed him. (Lk 15:20)
Wrath comes from a lack of power or a lack of wisdom or a lack of goodness and this lack is not in God but it is on our side. (LT 48)	How can I give you up; My heart recoils within me, my compassion grows warm and tender... for I am God not man... and I will not come to destroy. (Hos 11:9)

He does not have to forgive, because it is impossible for him to be angry. (LT 49)

Every good and perfect gift is from above, coming down from the Father of lights with whom there is no variation or shadow due to change. (Jas 1:17)

I saw that God is our true peace and he is our safe protector when we are in disquiet, and he constantly works to bring us into endless peace. (LT 49)

Grace, mercy and peace will be with us from God the Father and from Jesus Christ, the Father's Son, in truth and love. (2 Jn 3)

THE SERVANT & THE LORD

Julian on some occasions may have seen a mystery play. Some scholars[2] have in fact suggested that she did and that the one which had impressed her most contained an actor who was dressed up as a noble lord and one who was in torn and ragged clothes. This second character, who seemed to be a servant, was, the scholars speculate, commissioned by the lord to do some very special task but, in his hurry to obey, he fell! Perhaps he did so through some kind of trapdoor in the platform which had been erected as a stage. In any case those who had gathered to enjoy the play may well have at that moment gasped, or laughed.

A little later, that same servant may have reappeared. If so, on this occasion he may have been dressed in splendid robes to indicate that he had been rewarded for the effort he had made. We can, of course, but speculate about the details of a play which Julian, perhaps, had seen. But what we know for certain is the way that she described the one which, at some moment in her 'great experience', began to float across her mind. She, certainly, was very much intrigued by what she saw. However she was puzzled too and wondered what that mental-play of hers could mean.

It was within her second book that Julian described this 'play' for us which she in fact had pondered for so long. She said that she had seen in it a 'lord' who gave instructions to a 'servant' but she mentioned then one detail which may not have been in any mystery play which she had seen. It was that, as he told the servant what to do, he gazed at him 'most lovingly'. Then, as she spoke about the servant who had hurried off to do all that his lord desired, she intimated that he, too, was acting in a very loving way. There, consequently, was in each of them a great love for the other and that love was not diminished even though the servant fell into a hole and what the lord desired did not seem to be done.

Julian reflected on this play, or picture-parable, but for a long time she did not know what it meant. The images of servant and of lord, which at that moment must have bubbled up from her subconscious, did not seem to harmonise with what she thought they ought to represent. The servant, for example, seemed too good to represent herself, a sinner[3] who in many ways continued to fall short of what she wished to be. Nor, for that very reason, did he seem to symbolise the human race itself, although he might have been called Adam in the mystery play which we have presupposed. Who then, she kept on wondering, could he be? Indeed, if Julian had not been so persistent in her efforts to resolve this mystery, he, and all the other details of the story which contained him, might have disappeared like some unwanted dream. But she was not the kind of person to let such a thing occur.

For up to twenty years she struggled with this graphic story of the servant and the lord.

We do not know exactly when the penny dropped but it was after she had finished her initial book and even later than a first edition of her second one. In any case, she came at last to realise that that good servant in her picture-parable could be in fact considered of as a symbol of the human race (and therefore of herself as well). However, let us note that this seems to have happened only as she found that she could think of Christ himself, not as some kind of noble lord as she had done, but as a struggling person like us all. The servant-figure in her picture-parable was consequently recognised to be an image of both him and all the rest of humankind in its relationship to God. His plight was able then to signify for her the sufferings of everyone, including those of Christ himself, while his sheer goodness was, not only the expression of the kind of person which she longed to be but also a portrayal of what had in fact been realised in him who was to be eventually raised on high. Of course, the implication was, that with his help, she too and all the other members of the human race could grow into that goodness too.

Having solved the problem of the servant, let us focus for a moment on that other figure which was in her picture-parable, that of the noble lord. If it should not be understood as representing Christ, as she had thought, then who, she must have often wondered, could he be? The answer, which of course she quickly found when she discovered that the servant represented humankind, was that he was that ever-loving Father who sees Christ and all of us as one.

This understanding of her picture-parable led Julian towards a very definitely trinitarian awareness. She began to see her own relationship with Christ within the context of the one which he had with his Father and with all those other people whom the Father gave so lovingly to him. In consequence, she looked again at all those 'Showings' which she had already pondered for so long and, when she did, she found in many of them certain aspects which she had not noticed up till then. However, we have had an opportunity to note a number of those aspects as we went along, so let us simply recognise again how much her understanding of the roles played by the Father, Son and Holy Spirit in our own development changed her from being just a somewhat pious individual into a person with a message which was valid for all Christians everywhere. She grew, indeed, into that person who can still help everyone to see themselves as totally accepted by a loving Father, since they are already one with Christ his Son, and in the Spirit able to accept all others in anticipation of that perfect unity to come.

In the sight of God all human-kind is one. (LT 51)

In him all things were creat-ed… in him all things hold together. (Col 1:16-17)

When Adam fell, God's Son fell; because of the true union which was made in heaven, God's Son could not be separated from Adam, for by Adam I understood all humankind. (LT 51)

For as in Adam all die, so in Christ all live. (1 Cor 15:22)

Now the Son… stands be-fore the Father with a rich and precious crown upon his head. (For it was re-vealed that we are his crown). Now he sits at the Father's right. (LT 51)

The last Adam became a life-giving Spirit. (1 Cor 15:45)

When all things are subjected to him, then the Son himself will be subjected to him who puts all things under him, that God may be all in all. (1 Cor 15:28)

THE MYSTERY WITHIN

Julian was conscious of a depth within herself. It was a depth which constantly attracted her although it also always stayed beyond her power to plumb. In fact she found it easier to say what it was not than to explain exactly what it was.

It was not, for example, that part of herself which could be-come upset when life demanded more of her than she expected or which on occasions could be filled with sorrow or with woe.[4] That part of her was very real indeed but Julian, it seems, was able to accept it as an 'outer part'[5] and to believe that under-neath it there was still another and a more important one. Those worries then were only like the waves which, even though they might at times be strong and terrifying, did not mean that far below them there was not a mighty depth of calm and silent sea. It was that hidden depth which she was indicating when, refer-ring to her 'inner part', she spoke about a blessed life within herself which she had secretly experienced.[6] But more than that she did, or could, not at that moment say.

However, let us note again that when she spoke about that 'inner part' she did so in connection with discovering that she in fact could do what she would call her 'outer part' had no desire to do at all.[7] Of course, it may have been no more than just a way of speaking when, instead of saying 'I did such a thing', she spoke about her 'inner part' as being able to control and influence the 'outer one'. But, on the other hand, that way of speaking could have been occasioned by a sudden intuition of a power within herself which was, not only greater than her own but also one without which she could not have even tried to do whatever she had done. If so, what was that power? If somebody had asked her then, she might have answered that it was the power of love which, as we all know, can make people do extraordinary things.

It probably was when she came to understand her picture-parable that Julian began to think of this mysterious power within herself as Christ. Although the teaching of the church may have already told her that there was a unity between herself and Christ, her own appreciation of that teaching had to grow. So, it was only after years of pondering that she began to realise that she and Christ were one 'substantially' to use her chosen word. That means, it seems to me, that she believed that he was somehow in that 'inner part' which is within us all, and that in consequence he can reach out and influence the 'outer part' of each of us, which she at this stage calls our 'sensuality'. Thus, in her own case, when she had in some way actually helped another person, and especially perhaps when doing so had not been easy, she would afterward have been convinced that it was Christ within her who had reached out through her with a loving power which otherwise she never would have had.[8] It, consequently, must have been with awe and gratitude that in her quiet moments she would marvel at that growing and transforming Christ-dimension of herself.

Julian continued in her later life to marvel at this mystery and, from time to time, to ponder it as well. In consequence, she came to see, not only that she was, with Christ, enfolded in the love of him who is the Father of us all, but that she could become completely lost in that same love and, consequently, totally fulfiled. He is, she saw, the One who sees each one of us with that same act of seeing which saw Christ, just as he is the One who makes and saves each one of us with that same act which made and then exalted him. But Julian could leave those unifying thoughts aside when she was ready to relax and to allow her inmost self to merge with him who, in that same eternal act, can lovingly absorb us all. Indeed at such a moment she could sometimes feel so one with him that she no longer would be conscious of a barrier of any kind between herself and God.[9] That must indeed, have been a liberating and a marvellous experience, as well as being one which she presumed that all her future readers could have too.

God makes no distinction in love between the blessed soul of Christ and the least soul that shall be saved. (LT 54)

O righteous Father... I have made known to them your name so that the love with which you have loved me may be in them. (Jn 17:25-26)

Where the blessed soul of Christ is, there is the substance of all souls which shall be saved. (LT 54)

He destined us in love to be his children through Jesus Christ. (Eph 1:5)

It was to his eternal purpose to create human nature, which fair nature was first prepared for his own Son, the second Person; and when he wished... he created us all at once. (LT 58)

He (the Word) was in the beginning with God; all things were made through him and without him was made nothing that was made. (Jn 1:2)

Your life is hid with Christ in God. (Col 3:3)

I saw no difference between God and our substance but, as it were, all God. (LT 54)

His divine power has granted all things that pertain to godliness that you may become partakers in the divine nature. (2 Pet 1:3-4)

THE TAMING OF THE OUTER PART

Julian was interested in bringing what was separate together. She herself appears to have been someone who possessed a high degree of integration in herself and it would seem that she did all she could to help a lot of others to acquire the same. No doubt, in doing so, she helped a number of those people to relate to others in a better way as well. However, if she did, it is quite clear that, for herself, becoming integrated as a person was a process very closely linked with an ability to let herself become enfolded in the presence of the One who can give harmony to all. God was, she knew, the certain source from which the peace and happiness which all of us desire can flow.

If Julian desired all people to be influenced by this enfolding presence she was also very conscience of those inclinations, even in herself,[10] which tend to go in different directions and to drag us in their wake. At times, such knowledge may have made her feel a bit depressed, if not despondent, but, in spite of that, she was convinced that all the bits and pieces of our lives which worry us can be collected into that deep growing unity which she at other times could secretly experience. Indeed, to use again her earlier expression, she was sure that her own 'inner part' was able with the grace of God to draw her wayward 'outer part' into agreement with itself.[11]

But let us pay particular attention to her words. She did not say that her own 'inner part' should fight or try to overcome her 'outer part' but simply that it had a power to draw it to itself. That seems to indicate that she preferred to deal with her own wayward 'outer part', not in the manner of St George who killed the dragon which he did not like, but in a way which was more patient and much more effective too. Indeed her attitude was similar to that which was attributed to Martha in another legend of those medieval days. That lady also met a dragon, we are told, but, when she did, she used no violence but, by treating him with kindness, neutralised the danger which he posed and subsequently tamed him so that he became a seemingly, domesticated friend.[12] Was that a feminine approach or one which could be thought of as maternal or, much more profoundly, was it God's own Spirit working through her in that kind of way?

In this connection let us note that, while there can be little doubt that Julian did all she could to draw her wayward 'outer part' towards the peaceful centre of herself, she was in fact convinced that, as that happened, it was really being done by someone who was greater than herself. Her picture-parable, when she had come to understand its meaning, made her realise that Christ was one-with-her and so it also made her very much aware that, as she tried to tame those loose ends of her personality, her efforts were corroborated by his own. Indeed she realised that even her desire for inner harmony and peace was being all the time infused with his own 'godly will'[13] and, therefore, she was certain that her prayer for integration would be heard. Of course, there were, and would be, moments when that did not seem to happen but, since she believed that Christ himself accepted her just as she was, she could continue to accept her wayward parts with equanimity and hope. The very fact that he was actually dwelling in her 'inner part' empowered her to continue caring for those 'dragon' elements which she discovered in herself and to believe that, with his grace, they would be tamed and integrated into her maturing personality.

There was one very homely image which, it seems, helped Julian to appreciate the sureness of this process which was taking place within herself and which, she knew, could take place in the lives of other people too. It was the image of a person knitting.[14] It can be, perhaps, presumed that normally a person knitting would have been a woman and that Julian would have observed how women knitting would create successive loops of wool and join them to the ones which were already made. No doubt, this was what Julian herself did many times when sitting in her anchorhold, although she does not mention such activity in either of her books. But, in those chapters which she added to her second one, she speaks of God as One who knits our different parts and, in the process, joins them both to Christ and, through him, to himself. Although it may have seemed to Julian that there was still a lot of unworked and confused material which had not yet become incorporated into the divine design, she realised that she had reason to relax. The patient and the careful Knitter would continue and complete the perfect pattern which he already had begun.

I saw and understood very surely that in each soul that will be saved there is a godly will which never assented to sin nor ever will... We have this blessed will whole and safe in our Lord Jesus Christ. (LT 53)

No one born of God commits sin; for God's nature abides in him and he cannot sin because he is born of God. (1 Jn 3:9)

It is the delight of Christ to reign blessedly in our understanding and sit restfully in our soul, and to dwell endlessly in our soul, working us all into him. (LT. 57)

We are to grow up in every way into him who is the head, into Christ from whom the whole body, joined and knit together by every joint with which it is supplied, when each part makes bodily growth and upbuilds itself in love. (Eph 4:15-16)

God wants us to know that the beloved soul of Christ was preciously knitted to him in its making, ... and that all the souls which will be saved in heaven are knit in this knot... (LT 53)

KIND MOTHERHOOD

When Julian spoke to those who came to visit her she did so in a way which may have taken many by surprise. She intimated, and at times explicitly declared, that it was right for them to think of God, and to relate to him, as they would to a kind and loving mother. That itself, it must be said, was not a new idea but, on the other hand, it probably was new to many of the peo-

ple who came to her anchorhold for help. Indeed, considering
the harshness of the world in which they lived, they were more
likely to have thought of him as male and even vengeful than as
one who overflowed with a maternal love. Nor would that understanding have been contradicted by the lives of many
churchmen or by their official statements which suggested that,
if God is love, he loves us only if we are prepared to do what he
commands. Within that context, then, the words of Julian must
have been a consoling factor for the lives of those who knew her,
as they have been for so many ever since.

Beginning, not from dogma, but from her own personal experience she spoke of God in ways which certainly were more
maternal than was normally the case. When, for example, she referred to clothes enfolding her[15] and intimated that they were a
sign of God, was she not indicating that he was a kind of womb
in which she could relax and, at the same time, find the warmth
and nourishment which she required? When, in a later chapter,
she declared that she had seen within the heart of Christ himself
a place in which there was sufficient room for all who would be
saved,[16] was she not indicating something which was fundamentally the same? I do not mean that by those early images she
was attempting to prepare us for a clearer statement to be made
some other time. She was, in fact, just trying to express that
sense of deep security which she had in her 'great experience'
and which she only later realised could be described in terms
which were explicitly maternal.

If a lot of people were attracted by the fact that Julian could
speak of God as if he were a mother (and because it is a thought
which she developed quite a lot, we can presume they were) it is
legitimate to wonder how it was that such a thought had managed to become so strong and meaningful as it so obviously did.

It would be tempting to consider here the influence which
Julian's own mother may have had on her when she was still a
child. However, all we know for certain of that lady is that she
was present when her daughter at the age of thirty-and-a-half
was very, very ill and that she tried to close her eyes when she

had seemed to die.[17] But, on the other hand, it could be argued that the kind of mother that she was is manifested in a lot of places in the books which that same daughter later wrote. One could, to be specific, claim that something of her personality shines through those passages which speak of God in a maternal way. Indeed, it could be asked: could Julian have spoken about God as both a loving and a caring mother with the deep conviction which she obviously had if she had not experienced in her own early days an earthly mother of that kind. Of course, we speculate. Yet Julian does seem to have developed into someone with a sense of deep security and that, in turn, seems to suggest that she was blessed with much affection and a lot of healthy care as she was growing up.

However, even if she had a kind and caring mother, it may not have been just her own personal experience of being mothered (that is, of receiving life) which influenced the way she thought of God, but her experience of giving life as well. It has already been suggested by some writers[18] that, before her 'great experience', she had in fact conceived and borne a child, a child which later may have died, perhaps in one of those recurrent outbreaks of the plague. But, even though she may have known what it is like to be a mother and, in consequence, to love a child as he or she was growing up, it must have been her own experience of spiritual mothering which really forced her to consider God as being in some way a loving mother too. In other words it may have been her own concern for those who trusted her which made her realise, not only that she could both nourish and then nurture them in their own spiritual growth, but, more importantly, that God could do so even more. Of course, that may have made her conscious of the value and importance of her contribution to their lives and, consequently, may have stimulated her to keep on making it. But it may have allowed her to relax as well. Just as her earthly mother may have given her the freedom which she needed for her growth, so she perceived that she could let those very people whom she wanted most to help to have the freedom which they needed to discover for themselves the Mother who alone could give them all which they desired, and would.

As Julian herself reflected on this powerful motherhood of God she realised that, since God is a Trinity, his motherhood had either to be something which concerned all persons of that Trinity or something which should be attributed to one. It is not too surprising that she chose the second option since tradition had already named one person of the Trinity as 'Father' and, in doing so, had made it difficult for him to be considered as a mother too. However, what may be surprising is that, having made that primary choice, she then linked motherhood in God, not to the Spirit which gives life (although in theory that could have been done) but to the One who is referred to in the scriptures as the Son.

Perhaps she had been influenced in this by certain medieval authors who already had considered Christ in a maternal way. St Anselm, for example, quoting scripture, had referred to him as one who, like the mother hen, would gather all the children of Jerusalem to keep them safe.[19] We do not know, however, whether Julian had been aware of that or of some comparable comment made by someone else but such ideas could have been fairly easily communicated to her through her spiritual guides. In any case, she did, not only speak of Christ as mother, but she did so with more emphasis than any other writer whom we know. She even urged all those who felt that they had soiled themselves in any way to run with confidence to him because he is that true and archetypal mother[20] who will, not just clean us from the stain of every sin, but also give us all the comfort we require.

I have heard certain Julian enthusiasts proclaim that she herself was a prophetic figure in the church and I believe that they are right. However, if that was in fact the case, it was not just because she spoke of God and Christ as mother or because she manifested in her own life such a motherly concern. It was as well and more importantly because, while doing that, she realised, and so proclaimed, an even greater truth. It was that God is more than mother, more than father too. The Deity for her, as we have seen, was neither 'he' nor 'she' but a transcendent 'it'.[21]

Indeed, it could be said that it was in surrendering herself completely to that awe-inspiring, if maternal, Deity that she herself was able to develop as she did. Moreover, it was, probably, because she had discovered for herself the One who is beyond all limitations that she was enabled to reveal so well that kind maternity which helped so many people of her time and nurtures many still.

As the child grows in age and in stature, she (the mother) acts differently, but she does not change her love. (LT 60)

You, O Lord, gave your people... bread ready to eat, providing every pleasure and suited to every taste. (Wis 16:20)

Our true mother Jesus, he alone bears us for joy and endless life. (LT 60)

These things I have spoken to you, that my joy may be in you and your joy may be full. (Jn 15:11)

I came that they may have life and have it abundantly. (Jn 10:10)

The mother can give her child to suck of her milk, but our precious mother Jesus can feed us with himself and does ... with the Blessed Sacrament. (LT 60)

He who eats my flesh and drinks my blood has eternal life and I will raise him up on the last day. (Jn 6:54)

Our courteous mother does not wish us to flee away ... but he wants us to behave like a child. For when it is distressed and frightened it runs quickly to its mother and if it can do no more it calls to the mother for help with all its might. (LT 61)

A weaned child on its mother's breast, even so is my soul. (Ps 130/131)

As one whom his mother comforts, so will I comfort you, says the Lord. (Is 66:13)

Notes

1. cf. Lk 15:20-24.
2. cf. Pelphrey, Brant, *Christ our Mother*.
3. Julian refers to herself as a 'sinful creature' in ST chapter 6 and in LT chapter 4 and hints from time to time at imperfections in herself.
4. cf. ST chapter 9 & LT chapter 15.
5. cf. LT chapter 19
6. ibid.
7. ibid.
8. cf. ST chapter 13 & LT chapter 28
9. Julian qualified her statement by declaring 'God is God and our substance a creature made by God' (LT 54). This was, no doubt, lest anybody should accuse her of proclaiming Pantheism, the belief that all is God, without distinguishing between life uncreated and created. But it is quite clear that Julian was much more interested in the experience of oneness which we all can have than in insisting on distinctions.
10. cf. 'we hate and despise our evil inclinations...' LT chapter 52.
11. cf. LT chapter 19
12. According to a Medieval Tradition, Martha of the Gospel story travelled in the south of France. There she was informed about a wild beast (also a dragon) which lived in a river and killed everyone who crossed. 'Martha went to oppose the dragon... poured holy water over it and held a cross in front of it, the dragon was subdued and stood there like a tame lamb.' Although the emphasis is that it is a woman who subdues the dragon (and although the dragon is eventually killed by all the local people) an important element of the story is that it was conquered without any violence. It was in fact subdued by Martha in what many would consider to have been a feminine, rather than a masculine or 'macho' way. (*Humanity in God* by Elizabeth Moltmann-Wendel. SCM Press Ltd, 1983). However, it should be noted that a similar, and even better, story is that of the wolf which was subdued by Francis of Assisi and, then, reconciled with those whom it had previously scared. (*The Little Flowers of St Francis* 21)
13. Julian mentions this 'good' or 'godly will' in ST chapter 17 and in the LT chapters 37, 53 & 59. It worried commentators for a long time, some declaring that at this point she had erred. (cf. Introduction to Clifton Wolters' translation). However, it seems preferable to consider it as the effective will of Christ in those who will, in fact, be saved.
14. cf. 'Man's soul is made by God and knit to God in that same point' 'He (God) wants us to know that this beloved soul (Christ's) was preciously knitted to him in its making, by a knot so subtle and so mighty that it is united in God... Furthermore, he wants us to know that all the

souls which will be saved are knit in this knot and united in this union and made holy in this holiness'. (LT chapter 53) 15. cf. ST chapter 4 & LT chapter 5.

16. cf. LT chapter 24.

17. cf. ST chapter 10.

18. cf. Ward, Sr Benedicta, *Julian Revisited*, a lecture referred to, with quotations in *In Search of Julian* by Sheila Upjohn.

19. cf. Lk 13:34.

20. Despite the imperfections of the church Julian could speak of it as 'mother Holy Church, who is Christ Jesus' (LT chapter 61). Although she did not say it was his body, her ecclesiology can be compared to that contained in the epistles to Ephesians and Colossians. However, the distinction which she made between an outer and an inner part would have allowed her both to cope with all its imperfections and to recognise that it contained an essence which is in itself divine.

21. cf. ST chapter 13 & LT chapter 26.

The 15th 'Showing' was about the yearning for a future and a better life which Julian experienced within herself and of her deep conviction that that yearning was inspired and so would be completely satisfied.

We are concerned with chapter 20 in the Short Text and with chapters 64 and 65 within the later, longer one.

CERTAIN HOPE

One of the gifts which Julian had prayed for in her early life was that of 'longing with her will for God'.[1] The others were 'contrition' and 'compassion' but it was the 'longing' gift which would give purpose to the other two while quietly disposing Julian herself for that great Gift of gifts for which we all are made. Of course, as we have seen, the very fact that she had prayed for such a 'rightful',[2] gift implied that it, to some extent, had been already given. Therefore, it is hardly too surprising to discover that, as she reflected on her 'great experience' in later life, this longing in herself could bubble, as it were, into a strong, beseeching prayer such as the one which we have had an opportunity to note. 'God of your goodness,' it began, 'give me yourself'.[3] Indeed that was a prayer which she may have repeated, even with increasing frequency, when all her writing was completed and indeed throughout the rest of her own earthly life.

But Julian also spoke about her longing as a 'wound'!

Already at that early age she had perceived that not to have what she desired could be itself a pain. To illustrate that with a simple everyday example we could say that, just as any child may cry because it cannot have the ice-cream or the cake that it desires, so Julian discovered, and discovered more and more, that there was pain in not possessing totally the God for whom her very nature longed. Indeed, in later years, when many ordinary things may have seemed less attractive than they had before, the one thing that her nature really yearned for, which was God, must have become for her at times more tantalisingly desirable. But, while he always seemed to stay so far beyond her reach and while her pain in not possessing him may have been mixed with physical discomfort as her body aged,[4] there is no evidence to indicate that Julian became despondent or depressed. From what she wrote,[5] she seems in fact to have succeeded very well in keeping her attention on the One who could, she knew, come suddenly and in allowing her desire for him, and for his totally transforming life, to grow.

There was, in this connection, one dramatic image which came to, or was it from, the mind of Julian and, consequently, helped her as she kept on yearning for that life of happiness to come. It was that of a little child emerging from a decomposing corpse and gliding with great liveliness to heaven. That she saw it coming from a decomposing corpse could have been caused by memories from early outbreaks of the plague when there were people dying everywhere and few who could provide for them a quick and decent burial. But such a vision could have also been a symbol of her own humanity which was in fact so close to death when she was thirty-and-a-half and which already was some decades older, if not ageing, as she laboured to complete her second book. The 'little child' in either context could have been a welcome and, indeed, a cheerful sign of hope. It could have symbolised, and even guaranteed, for Julian that life which she herself so much desired, a life which would not ever die but would be always open to the wonders of a world which she was sure would come.

As Julian reflected on that life which is to come, an allied thought passed quickly through her mind. It was that, as we wait for that great day when life will be completely new, we are not only individuals but people closely linked.[6] It is, of course, a pity that she did not catch that passing thought and tease it out in this place as she did in many others but the opportunity to do so was unfortunately missed. However, maybe we could say that once again her famous picture-parable would have assured her that this oneness which we have with one another as we patiently look forward to the happiness to come, is the result, not just of some supportive bonding, but of being by divine design part of the mystery of Christ. Indeed it is our solidarity with him which guarantees that what our deepest selves are longing for will one day be enjoyed. But it is also the result of being one with Christ that this deep oneness which we have with one another now will be, not only able to survive the decomposing power of death, but even able to enhance[7] the joy which each of us will have beyond.

So Julian continued to wait very patiently. She knew that some day in the future the eternal Father would take her, and all who will be saved, into the fullness of that life which Christ already has. She knew, moreover, that that moment when it comes will, not just last forever, but will also always have an unexpected tingle of delight. In her own words, it will not just begin but will be, as it were, 'beginning newly without end'.[8] Her longing was for that.

I saw a body lying on the earth, which appeared oppressive and fearsome and without shape or form; and suddenly out of this body there sprang a most beautiful creature, a little child, fully shaped and formed, swift and lively and whiter than a lily, which quickly glided up to heaven. (LT 65)

The earth was without form... And God said: 'Let us make humankind in our own image and likeness... And he saw that it was very good. (Gen 1:2, 26, 31)

Christ is the image of the invisible God, the first-born of all creation. (Col 1:15)

You will never again have pain of any kind, any kind of sickness, any kind of displeasure, any lack of your will (or wishing for what will in fact be disappointing!) but always joy and bliss without end. (LT 65)

God will wipe every tear from their eyes, and death shall be no more, neither shall there be mourning nor crying nor pain any more for the former things have passed away. (Rev 21:3-4)

God wants us to accept our sufferings as lightly as we are able, and to count them as nothing. For the more lightly we accept them, the less importance we ascribe to them because of our love, the less pain shall we experience from them and the more thanks and reward shall we have for them. (LT 65)

Count it all joy when you meet various trials for the testing of your faith produces steadfastness. And let steadfastness have its full effect, that you may be perfect and complete lacking in nothing. (Jas 1:2-4)

Notes

1. cf. ST chapter 1 & LT chapter 2.
2. cf. LT chapter 41.
3. cf. LT chapter 5.
4. Julian refers to bodily as well as to her spiritual pains in LT chapter 64.
5. Twice, in LT chapter 64, we find the formula 'It is God's will that we…' to introduce what we should do, be it to concentrate on that life which is still to come or to accept as lightly as we can the sufferings of this one. In both instances one does get the impression that, while Julian desired to do what she suggested, she was conscious that in fact she often failed.
6. Whereas in ST chapter 20 Julian had said that 'every soul, forgetting if he can the rest of creation, should acknowledge who it is who loves him' in her second text she changed that to a statement which was both more positive and focused on the bond we have among ourselves. She wrote 'God creates in us such a unity that, when it is truly seen, no one can separate himself (or herself) from another'. (LT chapter 65)
7. cf. ST chapter 9 & LT chapter 14.
8. What Julian actually wrote was: 'which new beginning shall last, without end new beginning'. (LT 63)

Part Five

A Living Faith

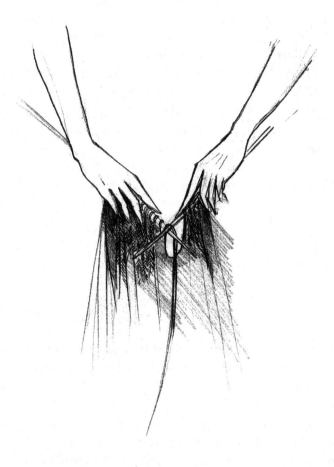

*We are to be knit together into Christ
who is knit into God*

After 15 'Showings' had been seen, there was a period of time before what was to be the final one. Within that period which lasted from mid-afternoon until the following morning, a succession of important happenings took place. The first seems to have been that Julian became more conscious of herself and of her physical condition. Secondly, she told a visitor, a 'person of religion', that she had been raving and went on to tell him all that had occurred. Then, she began to feel both guilty and depressed because that same religious person seemed quite ready to accept the life-restoring truths which she had been prepared so easily to doubt. A little later she apparently lay very still, no doubt considering what she should do, and then beginning to relax, she fell asleep.

At this stage the disturbing drama of her readiness to think of all those life-restoring truths as only products of a raving mind expressed itself symbolically in a dream. A devil seemed to hold her by the throat as if to throttle her and so deprive her of the very life which she so much desired. However, in her deepest self, she managed even then to put her trust in God and so the devil disappeared. Then Julian awoke and, even though she felt exhausted, she renewed her faith in all that had been manifested to her, both through her own personal experience and through the common understanding of the church. That act of faith resulted in a state of quiet peace and it was when she was in that condition that the 16th, and the final, 'Showing' was perceived.

We are concerned with chapter 22 of the Short Text and with chapter 68 within the longer one.

INDWELLING

Julian was conscious of a presence in herself.

She had been quite upset, indeed ashamed, because her conversation with the 'person of religion'[1] who had come to visit her had made her feel that she had doubted God's authentic revelation of himself. In consequence she went through a disturbing period in which she may have even felt that she could lose those very special blessings which she had so recently received. Indeed, if earlier the very thought that she might sin had worried her[2] the fact that she had actually done so caused her such upset that it expressed itself symbolically in a terrifying dream.

However, just as dreams no matter how upsetting pass, so too did her anxiety and Julian appears to have relaxed and to have found again a sense of inner peace and calm. That was for her a sign that God still loved her dearly and, moreover, that, through Christ, he was in some way actually dwelling in her too.

It would be interesting to know how much this change in her condition had been prompted by the celebration of the Resurrection which may even have been taking place at that same moment in the church which was beside her anchorhold.[3] I have suggested that the change which she had seen in Christ some hours before could have been caused by some improvement in her own condition, even though she realised that that improvement had itself been ultimately caused by the eternal source of overflowing life itself. Perhaps we now could say that her awareness of Christ living in her inmost self was also caused by some improvement in her physical condition as she wakened from that very troubled sleep. However, even if that was the case, a celebration of the Resurrection in the church beside her anchorhold could have effected, not her own recovery which came from that same source of overflowing life, but her perception of the risen Christ within herself which was its symbol and expression. Thus the liturgy which is both teacher and interpreter of life could have contributed in no small way to her own personal experience.

Julian, in any case, came to perceive, not just that Christ was risen but that he was very much alive in her. He seemed, indeed, to be like some great lord presiding in a stately place as many would, no doubt, have done in Norwich in those medieval days. He seemed, moreover, as she noted in her second book, to be a bishop too, a fact which certainly could have been caused by her remembering the grandeur of the local bishop, Lord Despenser, as he sat enthroned in his cathedral for the Paschal celebration or some other great liturgical event. Such images came easily to Julian's imaginative mind though obviously it was what they were suggesting to her that was the essential truth. On this occasion, it was that the Lord himself, now risen and exalted, was enthroned in her and consequently that, although she was a sinner and so insignificant, she was the sacred dwelling place which he had chosen as his own.

As Julian reflected on this life of Christ within herself, she was attracted by one detail of her vision in a very special way. It was that Christ was in a sitting posture in her soul. That posture, as she pondered it, seemed to suggest a state of rest and of contentment and, especially, a readiness to stay for evermore. Of course, while Julian rejoiced at such a constant presence in her life, she knew that it was possible to hinder its effectiveness in many, many ways. That was, indeed, what she herself had done a little while before. She, therefore, may have said to many of her visitors what she implied at this stage in the writing of her second book. It was that, if we were to let ourselves become more conscious of that powerful presence which is always in our 'inner part', we could allow it to control and tame our 'outer part' and so the quality of our own lives would be substantially improved.[4] Indeed, she even urges us towards a quiet contemplation of the Christ who is within us since, she knew, that such a contemplation can be most effective in allowing him to fill us with himself.[5]

It may be of some interest to recall in this connection one remark made by an old monk who was most unwilling to recite a certain prayer. The words in front of him apparently petitioned God not to withdraw his presence from our lives. 'But God does not do that', the old monk muttered with disgust and then began to search the book for some more orthodox alternative. I am quite sure that Julian would have approved. She knew that, while our sins can hinder God from doing all that he would like to do for us, he certainly does not do anything which is so negative as to 'withdraw'. However, in her case she would have been more conscious of the trinitarian dimensions of this very simple truth; she, therefore, would have been inclined to say that God, as Father, will not ever want to stop enfolding us within the Spirit of his love and that the reason is because he always sees in us the presence of his own beloved Son who is forever yearning to transform us more and more into the likeness of himself.

In the midst of that city sits our Lord Jesus, true God and true man, a handsome person and tall, highest bishop, most awesome king, most honourable Lord (LT 68)

It is no longer I who live but Christ who lives in me (Gal 2:20)

This was a delectable sight and a restful showing, which is without end and to contemplate it while we are here ... makes the soul which so contemplates like to him who is contemplated. (LT 68)

And we all beholding the glory of the Lord are being changed into his likeness from one degree of glory to another. (2 Cor 3:18)

He did not say: 'you will not be troubled, you will not be belaboured, you will not be disquieted', but he said: 'you will not be overcome.' God wants us to pay attention to these words and always to be strong in faithful trust. (LT 68)

In the world you will have tribulation; but be of good cheer, I have overcome the world. (Jn 16:33)

Notes

1. While it is possible that this religious person was a member of one of the male religious orders in the city, there is no reason to presume such membership. Some translators even say he was a parson.

2. cf. ST chapter 17 & LT chapter 37.

3. As already mentioned in a previous note, the 'great experience' of Julian could have occurred between Good Friday and the following morning when the Resurrection liturgy took place. That strange anticipation of the Resurrection liturgy in the early hours of Holy Saturday continued until the liturgical reforms of 1956.

4. cf. LT chapter 19.

5. Note what Julian wrote in ST chapter 22 & LT chapter 68: 'The soul who thus contemplates is made like to him who is contemplated.' This seem to be based on the thought that, while love draws us towards that which is loved, that which is known becomes part of the knower and, as such, improves or disimproves his or her own life.

The final chapters of the books of Julian concern the daily living of this love of God which her own 'Showings' had revealed. This can be difficult and she insists that we have much to do to stay within the vision of our faith. Indeed, she is prepared to speak about the ways in which she felt that she herself fell short of the ideal. Such a thought then leads her to discuss a form of fear which has to be rejected if we are to grow and then, in contrast, to insist upon another kind of fear which is, not only useful, but essential for us too. But, in the end, she has to leave us with the honest statement that there are two ways of viewing our success in life. However, as she does, there is no doubt as to the one which seemed to Julian herself to be the more important and the greater of the two.

We are concerned with chapters 23-25 of the shorter text and chapters 69-86 of the longer one.

LIVING IN FAITH

Julian was to live at least another forty years.[1] It was a period in which there would be no more 'Showings' even though there were, of course, the memories of those which she had had. To put that in another way she was, despite a privileged, if short, experience, the same as all her 'even-Christians' in not having more than just the ordinary light of faith to guide her through the challenges of life. It was, however, a sufficient light and one, moreover, which she knew God would provide and even measure out to her according to her need.[2] But Julian, was also very well aware that she herself had much to do in order to remain within that helping light and then to be transformed by all that it implied.

However, Julian did more than just recall the memories of her own 'great experience'. She did her very best to understand them in the broadest and most life-involving terms. No doubt she did that by discussing them with certain people whom she knew to be conversant with the prayer and faith tradition of the church and, probably, by sharing some with others whom she felt they might encourage or console. However, fairly soon, she came to realise that she perceived their meaning well enough to write her first and shorter book. That was a statement which, we know, would be expanded when she came to write a new edition and again when she decided to include some extra chapters in that second volume some years later still. But, while she laboured to compose those two books for the benefit of all her 'even-Christians', it was also a specific task which may have been of no small value for herself. It would have helped to keep alive for her the message of the 'Showings' which she had received and, consequently, it would have allowed that message both to influence her mind and than to guide her as she coped with each new situation as it came.

As Julian continued living day by day, enlightened only by the light of ordinary faith, she came to recognise the kind of situation which was likely to upset her and in which she easily could fall.[3] It was when God was trying to reveal himself to her in some way which was unattractive and which part of her would willingly ignore. That is in fact what had occurred when, in the context of her 'great experience' she had to overcome 'reluctance' in her 'outer part' and to allow that deeper and 'deliberate choice' which she discovered in her 'inner part' to lead her to the elevated cross.[4] In later life, of course, there must have been a number of occasions when that kind of struggle would have taken place in her again. To give a probable example we could say that there were surely times when she did not feel like proclaiming 'Deo Gratias', or 'Blessed be God',[5] when somebody disturbed her, even though her 'inner part' may often have been saying to her that she should. However, once she recognised the drama which was taking place within herself, she could at least begin to treat that weakness, or as she would say that 'sickness', which was in herself and which so easily could spread. She could for instance, and in fact she often did, recall the message of her 'great experience' and of her christian faith in general, and then allow the patient love of Christ, which was its central point, subdue the fever of her own impatience[6] with the way that God was organising life. Then once again she might discover that there was a truth in what she had so confidently at another time declared: that God works all things unto good.

But Julian was to become aware of one more sickness, or potential sickness, which in fact is even worse. It is a sickness
which is always able to develop from that little germ of doubt,
which can so easily be caught. When it develops it can make us
think, if only for a while, that God is not all-love, as had been
thought, and that he consequently does not have a super-plan
to make all that is not good to be well.

This was a sickness which had probably developed quite a
lot in many people when the Plague, the War and all the tur-
moil in society seemed to declare that God is anything but good
and full of loving care. Indeed, as Julian assures us, something
of that sickness can remain in even those who are, as she would
say, 'God's lovers',[7] and perhaps in saying that she was remembering that moment in her own life when the message of
her 'Showings' had appeared to her just too good to be true.[8]
So, once again, there seemed to her to be a need to find, and
then to trust, that basic instinct which is in us all and which both
echoes and confirms the fact that there exists, beyond all doubt,
a deity of constant and all-powerful love. The sixteen, very different Showings, which were Julian's own privilege to see, assured her that her own deep longing for that kind of God was
no mere fantasy or wishful-thinking in a world of sorrows but
the consequence of being actually loved by him who is Creator
of us all. It, therefore, was in drawing nourishment from all those
'Showings', and from her own Christian faith which had inspired so much of them, that she was able to control those crip-
pling and insidious doubts about God's loving nature which
can easily become a barrier for all of us to our own hoped-for
unity with him.

If Julian at certain times made quite an effort to retain the vision of her faith and if, in spite of that, she sometimes seemed to
fall, her underlying confidence in God as loving her allowed
her to continue to relax. Of course, as soon as she became aware
of any fault, she would have been unsettled by the wound of
true contrition, which was one of those three gifts for which she
had particularly prayed.[9] She would, moreover, have felt some

compulsion to confess whatever lack of patience she may have experienced as God was trying to direct her life and, as a consequence, whatever failing in compassion she may have been guilty of towards any of those very people who had come to her for help. Indeed, concerning what could be considered as her archetypal sin, that was her momentary doubting of the central message of her Showings, we could note that that fault was confessed, not only privately to some confessor as no doubt it was, but also publicly through what she wrote to all her future readers of her books.[10] But Julian who thereby learnt how to accept herself was also very sure that there can be a time when it is better to forget such failings and, instead, to let her mind become completely open to the ever-flowing love of him who willingly forgets our failings too.[11] Life in his love, appreciated in the light of faith, is all that she herself required. To use again some of her own terms here: it was enough to keep her seeking and, when necessary, waiting with a humble trust for all that, in accordance with her third petitioned gift, she longed so much to have and which, she knew, is promised to us all.

I set my eyes on the same cross in which I had seen comfort before, my tongue to speaking of Christ's Passion and repeating the faith of Holy Church. (LT 70)

Guard the truth which has been entrusted to you by the Holy Spirit. (2 Tim 1:14)

I thought privately to myself: Now you have plenty to do to keep yourself in the faith. ...accept (what has been shown to you), believe it and hold firmly to it, and comfort yourself with it and trust in it and you will not be overcome. (LT 70)

But you beloved, build yourselves up on your most holy faith; pray in the Holy Spirit; keep yourselves in the love of God. (Jude 20)

This is the victory that overcomes the world, our faith. (1 Jn 5:4)

God showed me two kinds of sickness that we have. One is impatience or sloth, because we bear our labour and our pain heavily. The other is despair or doubtful fear. (LT 73)

Some of us believe that God is almighty and may do everything and that he is all-wisdom and can do every-thing, but that he is all-love and wishes to do every-thing, there we fail. And it is this ignorance which most hinders God's lovers as I see it. (LT 73)

'Why are you afraid, O you of little faith' he said to them. (Mt 8:26)

God is love, and those who abide in love abide in God … In this is love made per-fect in us, that we may have confidence … there is no fear in love. (1 Jn 4:16-18)

A Place for Fear?

Fear is not a quality which one associates with Julian. She was a person who spoke freely about love and every sentence in her book reveals a woman who was happy in her inmost self and confident about the message she proclaimed. Yet one part of that very message was to say that fear can have a value for us too.

'Fear', however, may not be the best word to express what Julian had in mind. It can, and generally does, denote a feeling which is negative and, therefore, not what anyone would want. However, Julian herself was quite prepared to say that there are different kinds of fear and that, while there is one kind which will always hinder our development, there is another which is even necessary for a good relationship with God. The former is that fear which comes from doubting that the love of God is strong enough to bring us through whatever hardships we have to endure. It is in fact that second sickness which we have al-ready noted and which Julian, at times, could speak of even as despair. The other kind, however, is not only positive but liberating too. It is what Julian refers to as a 'reverential fear'.

A long tradition with its roots in scripture had already spoken of the 'fear of God' and had considered it as good but let us try to find some other and more useful words to indicate what that expression often meant. 'Respect' might be an option, even though to some it might be totally inadequate to indicate how someone should relate to him who is no less than the Creator of us all. The term which Julian suggested, namely 'reverence', is certainly a good one and, perhaps, it often is the best. But let us also mention 'awe', a word which we are likely to associate with those occasions when we sense a certain mystery which is marvellous or frightening, or perhaps in some way both. Have we at times not gazed with awe at the innumerable stars or at the raging of an angry sea? Have we not also felt a sense of awe in thinking about One who is so far beyond all thought that even 'God' can seem an insufficient word? However, while that kind of awe-like fear can have a value, it will never by itself make us respond to the Almighty One as Julian would have us do. A 'reverent fear', in other words, is good but it must always be accompanied by that deep knowing in the human heart that he who is so great is also loving us and, at the same time, helping us to love him in return.

Thus 'reverent fear' and 'love' belong to one another. 'They are brothers', to quote Julian herself, and they can, therefore, influence each other as we live our daily lives. For instance, 'love' in us, if it develops, can prevent its brother 'fear' from turning into something merely servile as can often happen, even in the case of people who are trying to be good. But, on the other hand, a 'reverent fear' in us is able to protect its brother 'love' from losing contact with the sheer immensity of God and so degenerating into something which, in fact, would be no more than just an interest in oneself. Indeed, the 'reverent fear' of Julian, both balanced and perfected by her selfless 'love', enabled her to marvel at the One who is so great and to be ready to obey him in whatever way he wished. Thus, far from thwarting her own fundamental love for him, that kind of fear allowed it to develop and to grow.

This 'reverent fear', moreover, will not ever end. It will remain in us, so Julian assures us, even in the realm of eternity itself. She knew that in its perfect form it will be hardly even noticed, so much will it be out-measured by the sweetness of authentic love. Yet, on the other hand, in speaking of a certain trembling[12] in the world to come, she indicates that there will be a very satisfying quality in our relating to the awesome and eternal God. It is that we will be, not only totally absorbed in his unending love, but constantly excited by the greatness of his majesty as well.

There is no fear in us which pleases God but reverent fear and that is gentle. (LT 74)

As the heavens are high above the earth, so strong is his love for those who fear him. (Ps 102/103)

Though our Lord revealed to me that I should sin, by me is understood everyone. And in this I conceived a gentle fear and in answer to this our Lord said: 'I protect you very safely'. (LT 37)

Work out your salvation with fear and trembling for God is at work in you both to will and to work for his good pleasure. (Phil 2:13)

Love and fear are brothers… It is proper to God's lordship to be feared; it is proper to his goodness to be loved. (LT 74)

The women departed quickly from the tomb with fear and great joy. (Mt 28:8)

I am sure that he who loves, he fears, though he may feel little of this. (LT 74)

Happy the one who fears the Lord and takes delight in his commands. (Ps 111/112)

The more it is obtained, the less it is felt, because of the sweetness of love. (LT 74)

O Blessed are those who fear the Lord and walk in his commands. (Ps 127/128)

This reverent fear is the fairer courtesy which is in heaven before God's face... by as much as he will be known and loved, surpassing how he now is, so much will he be feared, surpassing how he now is. (LT 75)

The angels, the elders, and the four living creatures fell on their faces before the throne and worshipped. (Rev 7:11)

MATTER FOR MEEKNESS AND FOR JOY

There is a two-part phrase which Julian liked to use when she was working on her second book. In chapter 79, for instance, she declared that there was *matter for meekness* in her own relationship with God and then went on to say that, from another point of view, she found that there was *matter for* much *joy* in it as well. In earlier chapters she had mentioned that same kind of contrast, even if she did use other words. Thus, when she had been talking about sin, she spoke of *matter*, not for meekness but for *mourning* and, indeed, for some *self-knowledge* too.[13] Then later, in another place, when she was pondering the nearness of the God who made us, she decided to present us with another and, indeed, delightful version for the second part of her well-balanced phrase. She said that she saw *matter* there, not just for joy (although that was included) but for *mirth!*[14] However, there was always that opposing contrast which, of course, is what we frequently experience in life.

Since life for Julian was, in its deepest sense, a love-relationship with God, it may be useful to recall that other love-relationship of which I briefly spoke. It was the one between a young Nigerian lady, whom I met, and her fiancé whom she liked to praise. It was, in fact, while she was actually doing that that she confessed that she felt totally unworthy of the love which he 'so obviously' had for her. In Julian's own terminology that much-loved lady had become aware of *matter for meekness* in herself and possibly, although she did not say so, of some matter in herself for *mourning* too. Yet, as she spoke, it was quite clear that she was also very happy. She was sure that she was loved. Despite her feeling of unworthiness, there was in her an even deeper feeling of contentment and of joy, the kind of joy, indeed, which seemed to guarantee to her more happiness to come.

All that was true for Julian herself in her own personal relationship with God. She knew that she did not deserve such a tremendous love and, as her life continued and her knowledge of herself increased, so did the depth of her conviction that she had good reason to be *meek* and frequently, to *mourn*. But, at the same time, she was also very happy in herself. The love of God, which she experienced in faith, made her aware of her inadequacies but it also indicated very clearly that she was, not just important, but of very special value too. She, consequently, was convinced that there was also *matter* in her life *for joy and even mirth as well*. Indeed, had she not, on occasions, laughed because all evil, even in herself, had been perceived as being overcome?[15]

Julian, however, would continue struggling with this paradox which living in the light of faith implies. She knew that she in many ways did not live up to her ideal yet she was convinced that she, and all of us, are loved by God as if we lived up to his own. Indeed when she came to compose the final chapters to her second book, which does not mean the last ones to be written, she would state the paradox again. *In our own eyes*, she wrote, *we seem to fall but, in the eyes of God, we seem to stand*. It may be of some value, therefore, to recall that well-known saying which declares that love is blind. It may be useful, too, to think again of that Nigerian lady who could say that, even if she felt unworthy, her fiancé was convinced that she was certainly the greatest thing that God had ever made. In any case there is no doubt that Julian was sure that God himself could see no sin in humankind[16] and, since his way of seeing us is better than the way we see ourselves, she knew that we could confidently try to make his point of view our own.

It was, of course, when Julian began to understand her picture-parable that she discovered how it is that God is able to accept us with approval and with love. It is because he sees us in conjunction with another and that other is none other than his own beloved Son. But, while that insight made it possible for her to understand how we can be so lovable, it did not make her sense of wonder or amazement any less. Indeed, it could have given her more *matter* for her *meekness* since it would have clarified how much was done for her and, maybe, it gave her more *matter for* her *mourning* too since it would have suggested just how un-enthusiastic her own personal response had often been. Yet, on the other hand, perceiving that she was substantially identifiable with Christ was *matter for*, not only *joy*, but also for much *mirth*, a mirth which ultimately came from him who welcomes everyone with his beloved Son into his ever-cheerful and eternal home.[17]

I have matter for meekness which saves me from pre-sumption ...and matter for true comfort and joy, which saves me from despair. (LT 79)	I saw the Lord sitting upon a throne. The seraphim called to one another saying: Holy, Holy, Holy... the whole earth is full of his glory. (Is 6:1-3)
	But my soul shall be joyful in the Lord and rejoice in his salvation. (Ps 34/35)
For we do not fall, in the sight of God, and we do stand in our own sight; both of these are true as I see it, but the way our Lord God sees it is the higher truth. (LT 82)	'Father, I have sinned against heaven and against you; I am no longer worthy to be called your son'. But the father said 'bring the best robe and put it on him...' (Lk 15:21ff.)
Then the Lord said this: See my beloved servant, what harm and injuries he has had... is it not reasonable that I should reward him? (LT 51)	He who raises the Lord Jesus will raise us also with Jesus and bring us into his presence. (2 Cor 4:14)

Let Us Pray

Julian let her book come to a relatively quiet end. She had al-ready shared all that she could and now she realised again that only God was able to communicate the rest.[18] She, therefore, was prepared to leave us with an invitation which, if we accept it, will bring us infallibly to him.

That invitation was quite simply 'let us pray'. However, since she knew that praying for what he who made us wants to give is always prompted and supporting in a loving way by him, she added to those words of invitation one short qualifying phrase: It was 'together with God's working'. Maybe she in later years[19] would have interpreted those extra words as indicating that, if we continue praying, God's own Spirit will be active in the evolution of our thoughts and in the growth of our desire. She certainly was sure that, in that Spirit, our own prayer can merge with that of Christ himself and that it, consequently, cannot but be heard. Her qualifying phrase can, therefore, re-assure us that, as we continue praying for the fullness of that life for which we yearn, the loving and involving dynamism of the Trinity itself will bring us on our way.

But let us also note that Julian, according to at least some manuscripts, may have been indicating that we should be able to rely on one another too as we pray for the life which has been promised to us all. To be precise, when she was giving us that invitation: 'Let us pray together with God's working', she may have been thinking 'let us pray together while, in his own way, God works through each of us'.[20] In some support for this more social understanding of her words, we could say that she probably told many of her worried visitors that she herself would pray for their intentions too. Moreover such a promise may in fact have been consoling to a number of those people since they would have known that she at least was absolutely certain that God listens to our prayers. Perhaps it is the same for those who know that we remember them and, maybe, we for our part often feel in no small way supported by the prayers of certain people as we keep on diligently searching for the One who is beyond all others and who can fulfil our deepest and most lasting needs.

This search, however, is a personal and often, in what could be thought of as the best sense of the word, a 'lonely' one as well. If Julian, for example, both encouraged and supported many people by her presence and her prayer, there can be little doubt that she stayed for the most part of each day alone within the confines of her anchorhold. Moreover, everything she wrote implies that she was certain that if all her future readers were to spend a little time, perhaps each day, within their spiritual anchorholds, that is within themselves, they too would find that fundamental yearning which could guide them, as it can guide all of us, towards that totally transcendent One who can fulfil us with himself. She knew, however, that as we allow that fundamental yearning in ourselves to influence our prayer and everything we do, we will in fact begin to be affected by that endless life which God will give his own beloved ones. Indeed, like Julian herself, we will begin already in this present world to be what that aloneness can suggest, that is 'all one'[21] within ourselves – and so, perhaps, a sign to many others of a love which can unite, and even totally transform, us all.

From the time that it was revealed, I desired many times to know in what was our Lord's meaning. And fifteen years after and more, I was answered in spiritual understanding, and it was said: 'What, do you wish to know our Lord's meaning in this thing? Know it well, Love was his meaning. Who reveals it to you? Love. What did he reveal to you? Love. Why does he reveal it to you? For love. Remain in this, and you will know more of the same. But you will never know different, without end.' (LT 86)

God is love, and the one who abides in love abides in God and God abides in such a person too. (1 Jn 4:16)

Notes.

1. There is a late introduction to the Short Text which proclaims: 'Here is a vision shown by the goodness of God to a devout woman, and her name is Julian, who is a recluse at Norwich and still alive, A.D. 1413, in which vision are very many words of comfort, greatly moving for all those who desire to be God's lovers.'

2. cf. LT chapter 83.

3. cf. LT chapter 73.

4. cf. LT chapter 19.

5. 'Blessed be God' or some similar phrase was an expression often used by Julian and one which indicates her basic attitude of soul.

6. cf. LT chapter 10 & 73.

7. cf. LT chapter 73.

8. cf. ST chapter 21 & LT chapter 66.

9. cf. ST chapter 1 & LT chapter 2.

10. cf. ST chapter 21 & LT chapter 66.

11. 'Just as by God's courtesy he forgets our sins from the time that we repent, just so does he wish us to forget our sins and all our depression and all our doubtful fears' (ST chapter 24) Note, however, that this sentence from the Short Text, while emphasising what we ought to do, is not as accurate regarding God's immutability as she can often be. For instance, Julian implied in LT chapter 49 that God does not have to forget our sins since he does not have to begin forgiving them, never having blamed us in the first place. In other words such change is not in God.

12. 'This kind of trembling and fear will have no kind of pain but it is proper to God's honourable majesty so to be contemplated by his creatures, trembling and quaking in fear because of their much greater joy, endlessly marvelling... Therefore, it must necessarily be that all heaven, all earth will tremble and quake...' (LT chapter 75)

13. cf. LT chapter 36.

14. cf. LT chapter 72.

15. cf.LT chapter 14.

16. Apart from seeing Christ in us, we could recall that Julian on one occasion could declare: sin is itself 'no thing'. (cf. ST 11)

17. 'I saw him reign in his house as a king and fill it all full of joy and mirth, gladdening and consoling his dear friends with himself.' (cf. LT chapter 14)

18. 'I trust in our Lord God almighty that he will, out of his goodness and love for you, make you accept it more spiritually and more sweetly than I can or may tell it.' (LT chapter 9)

19. I am presuming here that Julian composed this final chapter to her

second book before she came to understand the picture-parable of the Servant and the Lord and so before her thought became so Trinitarian as afterwards it did.

20. 'Pray we all together with God's working'. If 'together' is connected with the exhortation 'let us pray' one can accept this corporate interpretation. However, it must be admitted that the word 'together' which is in one of the early manuscripts (P), is not found in the other major ones (S1 & S2).

21. The word 'alone', according to the *Oxford English Dictionary*, comes from the adverb 'all', and the substantive 'one'. If its meaning is invariably that of being separate from others, there is no intrinsic reason for excluding one which indicates the psychological or spiritual oneness which such separation can at times facilitate.

Biblical Quotations

Suggested Bibliography

Texts of Julian's works:
Revelations of Divine Love, Clifton Wolters, trs, Penguin, 1985.
Showings, Colledge & Walsh, trs, The Classics of Western
        Spirituality Series, SPCK, 1978.
A lesson of Love, Father John-Julian, trs, DTL, 1991.

Selected Snippets from Julian:
Enfolded in Love, DLT.
In Love Enfolded, DLT.

Studies:
In Search of Julian, Sheila Upjohn, DTL, 1989.
Julian, Woman of our Day, Robert Llewelyn, ed, DTL, 1985.
Christ our Mother, Brant Pelphrey, DTL, 1989.
Julian of Norwich, Grace Jantzen, SPCK, 1987.
Julian's Way, Ritamary Bradley, Harpercollins Religious, 1992.